the
Hare

the Hare

Jill Mason

Photographs by David Mason

Merlin Unwin Books

First published by Merlin Unwin Books, Ludlow in 2005

Merlin Unwin Books
Palmers House
7 Corve Street
Ludlow
Shropshire SY8 1DB

www.countrybooksdirect.com

ISBN 1 873674 813

Designed by Think Graphic Design, Ludlow, Shropshire
Printed in Great Britain by Cambridge University Press, UK

To my husband David
who has been photographing wild hares for nearly twenty years.
His photos illustrating this book are the result of his skill and patience in
capturing the fickle nature of this free-spirited creature that has graced our
countryside for thousands of years.

Contents

Author's Note

My research into the common and latin names of the many species of hare in the world soon revealed that the subject is a disputed one, even among scientists. Naturalists and conservationists are not always in agreement about the correct nomenclature for hares, nor indeed on points of scientific definition. For example, the Varying hare is sometimes described as the Mountain hare, the Snowshoe hare and the Arctic hare. In turn the Snowshoe hare is known in the USA as the Snowshoe rabbit (or jackrabbit). And there are many other hare species which go under various different names, or are known by different names in different parts of the world, or according to different scientific authorities. In this book I have tried to go with those names and definitions that seem to be most widely accepted. I am not a zoologist, so if despite my research I have made errors they are mine alone and I hope they are not misleading.

During the final stages of the publication of this book the Hunting Act has been passed by the British Parliament and this affects some of the information in Chapter 11. However, because the Hunting Act, at the time of going to press, is the subject of a legal challenge by the Countryside Alliance, and because the ancient history of hunting the hare is a matter of general interest, I have decided to leave Chapter 11 as originally written.

Jill Mason, November 2004

Introduction

There is something special about a hare.

Many people can't tell a hare from a rabbit, but those who *can* make the distinction, often become charmed by this weird animal whose behaviour can defy all logic. The hare even seems to have the power to turn some perfectly normal individuals into complete hare fanatics!

So what is the attraction of this enigmatic creature? Is it because this timid animal has such large eyes which give no clue about its feelings? Maybe it is the hare's erratic behaviour which fascinates man. Or perhaps the relationship between man and hare goes back even further. In today's secular age, does the hare still have the capacity to stir our spirit, our sense of mystery, as it did our ancestors?

1

In culinary terms, in Britain at least, the hare must be pretty near the bottom of the list. Unlike pheasant, partridge, grouse, venison or even wild boar, the hare only rarely appears as an up-market pub speciality and is certainly an unusual item on restaurant menus.

The hare is far more favoured for its sporting potential. It is an animal that provides a challenge especially for those with hounds who enjoy seeing a hare pitting its wits and speed against those of their dogs.

Like most keen field sportsmen, hunting people are usually interested in the behaviour of their quarry and become knowledgeable about it. Those who spend their time watching hares in the wild can bear witness to happenings from which the folklore and superstitions of long ago were born. Beagle and harrier followers have witnessed the inexplicable disappearance of a hare when the pack is close on its trail.

Why does this creature with more speed than a hound and with equal stamina, suddenly stop running, clap down and remain crouched, close to the ground? This is just one example of the hare's uncanny 'wisdom'. It may be visible to the eye of a man when it lies low but on a day when scenting conditions are bad, it can prove invisible to a hound that sees with its nose but not its eye. While the scent in the air may be strong enough to indicate that a hare is close by, a dog may even unwittingly tread on the hare in its effort to pin-point the position.

Unless there is movement a hound does not use its eyes. But other species of dog hunt by sight and not scent. Greyhound and saluki enthusiasts will also bear witness to how easily a hare can escape. It is, however, far more difficult for a hare to elude a lurcher for this species will use both his eyes and his nose.

Not many British people gain much pleasure from shooting a hare. The shooter who has failed to place his shot accurately and only wounded one will give testament to the blood-curdling scream emitted by the injured animal. It is a haunting sound that stirs the emotions and must have put great fear into the gullible minds of people who believed in witches and evil.

It is hardly surprising that such a mysterious nocturnal animal should have imprinted itself so strongly on people's

Opposite
The countryside would be a poorer place without this curious creature, the Brown hare

minds in days long ago. Superstitions relating to hares abound and references to them in folklore throughout the ages are prolific. Many different names have been bestowed upon them.

Hares have been around for many centuries. The Greeks, Persians and Egyptians recorded their presence and there is even mention of them in the Bible. Writers including Shakespeare, Goldsmith, Yeats, Burns and Kingsley have mentioned the hare in all kinds of contexts. The poet William Cowper (see page 175) even kept a hare as a pet.

In the seventh century, before Christianity spread across Britain the hare was held in high regard by the pagans but because of its association with them it was ostracised by the new religion. The hare was part of pagan celebrations to mark the arrival of Spring. This springtime worship of the hare was re-invented by the Christians who substituted the Easter Bunny.

The hare has always been highly valued by sculptors and painters as a subject for art. It is a creature that stimulates the imagination, and the hare can be portrayed in many different guises: perhaps in a natural position, true to life, crouched down or sitting with ears erect. Some artists choose to emphasise its

Right
Brown hare on full alert in a stubble field

Below
At a glance, the Mountain hare can look very much like the rabbit but their behaviour is totally different

raw-boned frame, its long legs, its large ears. Others prefer to capture the hare when it stands on its hind legs, behaviour which would probably have greatly unnerved our ancestors who knew of no other animals which, like man, could move about on two legs with such agility. Many sculptors impressions of hares may border on the realms of fantasy.

More than 500 years ago the German Renaissance artist, Albrecht Dürer, painted a small watercolour titled 'A Young Hare' which is a brilliant portrayal of the Brown hare, just as we know it today. Caricatures or cartoons of hares were a part of many people's childhood, appearing on the pages of *Alice's Adventures in Wonderland* as the March Hare and on the screen as Bugs Bunny (hares are called jackrabbits by the Americans).

There can be few other animals about which so much is known but which still remain a mystery. Researchers may have recorded what hares do, but they are far from knowing everything about why they do it.

Various species of hare can be found right across the world from America, throughout Europe and Asia to Japan and from the Arctic to South Africa. They were not native to South America, Australia and New Zealand but were introduced. Different species of hare have evolved to cope with a range of environments and each strain is individually adapted to living in such diverse conditions as dry deserts, cold mountains or the arable lands of the Northern Hemisphere.

The Mountain hare has always been in Britain, even longer than man, but opinions differ as to when and how the Brown hare arrived on the scene. Some say it crossed from Europe long ago when a land bridge connected Britain to the Continent. Others suggest that the Romans, when they invaded, brought the Brown hare with them for food and for sport: certainly evidence exists to show that hares have been hunted with dogs for thousands of years.

In Britain the population of Brown hares has declined during the last century, theories abound as to why numbers have dwindled. In some parts, particularly the east of England, they still thrive but in others they have all but disappeared.

For most of the year the hare is a reclusive animal remaining

Some differences between hares and rabbits

- rabbits are smaller, have shorter ears, closer coats
- rabbits are more grey than hares
- rabbits are gregarious while hares are solitary
- rabbits prefer the margins of fields, hares the open ground
- rabbits inhabit burrows, hares live above ground
- rabbits are born naked and blind, hares are born fully furred and with their eyes open

more or less unseen but at times, jack hares have the habit of throwing every bit of caution to the wind, acting very strangely and making their presence blatantly obvious. This behaviour is most often seen in Spring and has given rise to the theory that hares go mad in March, but it is in fact part of their courtship. Anyone who has witnessed this boxing and fighting will probably never forget the sight.

There are many people in this country who find it difficult to tell a Brown hare from a rabbit and yet no two animals, so closely related, could behave so differently. They both belong to the group of animals known as lagomorphs, but that is where the similarity ends. Rabbits are smaller and have much shorter ears. Their coats are closer, more grey in colour and do not have the longer guard hairs that are particularly noticeable in a hare's winter coat. Even though they are smaller, rabbits can be aggressive to hares. Rabbits are gregarious animals that live in

The rabbit (*Oryctolagus cuniculus*) is superficially similar to the hare but in terms of its behaviour it is very different

holes in the ground and come out to feed at dusk. They do not often venture into the middle of fields, preferring the margins, and at the slightest hint of danger they run back to their burrows with the white underside of their tails showing as a danger signal. Rabbits tend to nibble crops very close to the ground, mainly around the edges of fields adjoining hedges, woodland or clumps of trees.

They have their babies underground often at the end of a freshly dug-out burrow in a nest lined with dried grass and fur pulled from their chests. The young rabbits are born naked, blind and helpless and the doe returns at night to feed them. On departing she fills the entrance to the burrow with soil so that

Below
Male and female hares 'boxing' in early Spring. The hare's odd behaviour has fascinated humans for centuries and only recently are we beginning to understand what lies behind displays like this

there are no obvious signs that there is a litter of babies inside. Rabbits in large numbers become a serious pest and do a great deal of damage by eating crops, including young trees and shrubs, and digging holes in the ground.

On the other hand, Brown hares are mainly solitary creatures which generally only come together either to feed or mate. They live on top of the ground right out in the open.

Their only defence against danger is to crouch down and rely on the camouflage of their coat or to run away, which they can do at great speed. When a Brown hare runs it carries its tail downwards so the white underneath doesn't show.

Young hares are called leverets which is thought to have been derived from the French word 'lievre' which means hare. Leverets are born fully furred with their eyes open and are very soon capable of running. No proper nest is built and after a day or so the doe spreads them out, leaving them hidden on their own in different places, from which they do not move. Their sole protection is to keep very still if they are threatened. The doe only returns for a few minutes during the night to suckle them.

Danger abounds, not only from predators but also from modern farm machinery which means that young hares are

Above
A cautious approach! Brown hares are solitary creatures for most of the year. To see them interacting in groups during the day only occurs when they are drawn towards a good food source or to a mate in Spring

extremely vulnerable when the crops they hide in are cut. Wet weather and disease can also take their toll. Most farmers like to see a few hares on their farms for they don't cause the damage that rabbits do.

Hares were once a common sight across the country but not any more. Within proposals in the British government's Bio-diversity Action Plan (BAP) it is hoped that the population of Brown hares in Britain can be doubled by 2010. However, this will be extremely difficult to implement.

In a few areas hares are still over-abundant and it is necessary to conduct an annual cull to reduce numbers both for the protection of crops and woodland and also the welfare of the hare itself. Over-crowding is a recipe for disaster. In other places, mostly on the western side of the country, hares are now a rare sight. At face value it would be logical to catch them up in regions where they are numerous and relocate them to areas where they are scarce But until the reason is found as to why their numbers have declined so rapidly in the first place and these problems addressed accordingly, this would prove to be nothing more than a short-term fix.

Hopefully the BAP scheme will be successful in finding solutions to the bigger problems and the mad March hare will once again be seen dancing on his hind legs in all of our green pastures.

The British countryside is a much poorer place without this curious creature.

In Pagan times the hare was a sacred animal. This modern sculpture by Michael Watts portraying a hare with a Celtic cross is on display at the church dedicated to St Melangell, patron saint of hares, at Pennant Melangell in north Wales

Hares of the World

The subject of hares is a much disputed one. The only thing you can be certain about is that you can't really be certain about anything.

Some early naturalists termed the hare family *Dasypoda* which in Greek signifies that they are hairy-footed. Until 1912 rabbits and hares were classified as rodents but subsequent study proved them to be of a different order called *Lagomorphs*. This not only includes hares and rabbits but also pikas. Hares and rabbits belong to the family of *Leporidae* and pikas to *Ochotonidae*. Opinion is greatly divided as to how many actual species of *Lagomorphs* there are. Figures vary from 14 to 25 species of pika and 40 to 53 rabbits and hares.

No doubt this discrepancy can be partially explained by the

An adult Brown hare, perfectly camouflaged in its arable setting: this and speed are its only defences

11

number of sub-species and whether they are counted separately; and by the fact that there seems to be an overlap in differentiating hares from rabbits. It poses the question: when is a hare not a hare? - and it seems that even the experts are uncertain on that one.

Opinions differ as to whether the Corsican hare (*Lepus corsicanus*) found in southern Italy, Sicily and Corsica is a distinct species, a sub-species of the Cape hare (*Lepus capensis*) or the Brown hare (*Lepus europaeus*) or the result of interbreeding. Modern scientific research using, amongst other things, DNA testing has added to the confusion by discovering that the Corsican hare is probably more closely related to the Mountain hare (*Lepus timidus*). The population of the Corsican hare has seriously decreased since World War II through over-hunting and the introduction of the non-indigenous Brown hare.

The Latin names given to any species of creature can be very confusing, especially with hares. Henry Tegner deals with the matter quite lucidly in his book *Wild Hares*. To paraphrase, in the order of animals, a hare is a *Lagomorph*. It is of the *Leporidae* family and its genus is *Lepus*. Next classification is the

Right
The Scottish Mountain or Blue hare in winter coat (*Lepus timidus scoticus*)
The Mountain hare in Britain turns white in winter

Below
The African or Cape hare (*Lepus capensis*)
80 sub-species of *Lepus capensis* are known to exist. They are found in desert and grassland areas across many parts of Africa, southern Europe, Arabia, central Asia and eastern China

species, eg. *timidus* (Blue/Mountain hare) or *capensis* (Cape hare). After that follows the sub-species, eg. *scoticus* (Scottish Mountain hare) or *hibernicus* (Irish hare). Things are often further complicated when the surname of the person who has taken credit for identifying the sub-species is tacked on the end, such as the desert-living Sand hare of Arabia, *Lepus capensis cheesmani*.

It appears that hares were originally indigenous only to the northern hemisphere and Africa but, because they have been introduced elsewhere over the centuries, they are now present on every continent except Antarctica.

Above
This diminutive Northern pika can be found at high elevations across North America, Siberia, China and Japan. It is sometimes called a Mouse hare or a Whistling hare, although it is only a distant relative. Pikas are much smaller than hares and there are many different species of them in the northern hemisphere

Characteristics of all hares

All species of hare have similar characteristics, but with subtle differences. They normally live above ground although a few will seek shelter from extreme conditions or take refuge in holes or short burrows, usually dug by other creatures. They are generally (but not always) nocturnal and solitary by nature, and they may travel considerable distances to find high quality food. Hares, like rabbits, pass two kinds of droppings. One kind is soft and moist and is eaten so that the food passes through the digestive system for a second time before being expelled as dry fibrous faecal pellets. Coat colour can vary greatly within a species but all hares are some shade of brown with the exception of the Black jackrabbit and the Manchurian Black hare. A few of the northern species such as the Snowshoe hare and White-tailed jackrabbit and the Arctic, Mountain and Japanese hares turn from brown to white in winter.

All hares rely on camouflage and speed for their survival and it is characteristic of the animal that when put to flight after running a distance they will stop and look round to ascertain where the danger now lies. Some species have been reported as reaching speeds of 50 mph (80km) and maintaining speeds of 30mph (50km) over long periods. All hares have long legs, large hearts and wide air passages for breathing and a lightly-built skeleton. The feet are covered with fur and there are five digits on the fore feet and four on the back. These physical characteristics enable hares to be agile and to run very fast.

Species of hares vary greatly in size and females are nearly always slightly larger than the males. Boxing, kicking and biting are associated with courtship behaviour. The gestation period varies between 35 and 50 days for the different species. Leverets are born fully furred with their eyes open and are mobile within a few hours of birth. In times of stress or poor nutrition, the foetuses are likely to be spontaneously reabsorbed.

When running, a Brown hare carries its tail downwards showing the black upperside. The rabbit, on the other hand, shows the white underside of its tail when it runs

Left
In the late 1950s and early 1960s Brown hares were sufficiently abundant in Hampshire as to make culling necessary.
This photo was taken outside the Peat Spade pub at Longstock, near Stockbridge, in 1965. Culls of this magnitude are a thing of the past, but the Peat Spade pub is still in existence to this day

Frequency of litters varies greatly with the climatic regions. Hare species living in the extreme north may only have one large litter of 6-8 babies each year while those close to the Equator may have up to eight litters a year but with only one or two babies at a time. Interestingly though, this still equates to an average of 8-10 young being born each year for all species world-wide.

Due to disease, weather conditions, malnutrition but most of all predation, it is likely that 90% of the young will die within their first year. The young are left unattended soon after they are born and the doe only returns to them at night to suckle them for a few minutes when it is dark. The population of many species shows noticeable fluctuations over a broad ten year cycle.

Vocal communication between hares is limited to occasional grunting and teeth-grinding. Thumping feet is

Above
An average total of 8-10 leverets are born to a doe throughout each year, although few will survive

Left
Baby hares are born fully developed. The Brown hare has three or four litters of two to four young a year. This larger than average litter of five are less than half an hour old

sometimes used as a signal and of course scent plays an important role. By far the loudest sound emitted by a hare is a piercing scream when it is injured or terrified.

Hares and the economy

For centuries hares have been of economic importance in many countries, providing meat and fur as well as sport. Before World War II they played an important part in the fur market. In Pre-revolutionary Russia, six million skins were sold annually by hunters. Pelts from the European Brown hare supplied 5.5% of the European fur market, and the Mountain hare about 6%. The fur was used extensively for the manufacture of felt and also for such things as trimming and lining gloves. Very few pelts are used today, as so many products of the fur trade have been displaced by man-made fibres and as a consequence, hare pelts have become of little value and therefore uneconomic to trade.

Endangered hares

According to the World Conservation Union (IUCN) 23 species of lagomorphs are threatened with extinction. Five species of rabbit and two of hare are at greatest risk. The endangered rabbits are the Riverine or Bushman rabbit (*Bunolagus monticularis*) from South Africa, the Volcano rabbit (*Romerolagus diazi*) found only in two volcanic sierras near Mexico City, the Amami rabbit (*Pentalagus furnessi*) that lives on two islands off the Japanese coast, the Sumatran Short-eared rabbit (*Nesolagus*

Below
A Polish woman selling hares. Early 1900s postcard. Even in 1976 the Brown hare was reported to be of economic importance in Poland with hunters killing about 700,000 annually

Above
The Mountain hare changing
from its white winter coat to its
brown summer coat

netscheri) from Indonesia, and the Tres Marias cottontail (*Sylvilagus graysoni*) from the Tres Marias islands, Mexico. The two hare species most at risk are the Hispid hare (*Caprolagus hispidus*) from India, Bangladesh and Nepal and the Tehuantepec jackrabbit (*Lepus flavigularis*) from Mexico.

Hares of various species are indigenous across the northern hemisphere and southern Africa. They live in America, Europe, Scandinavia, Asia, India, Africa, China, Russia and Japan. Although they aren't native to South America, Australia or New Zealand, they have been introduced there. As a general rule, the hotter an area a species of hare inhabits, the larger its ears are, for they act as a cooling mechanism.

Hare Identification

The identification of hares is a confusing subject because some species are no bigger than a rabbit while others are very large. It is said as a general rule that hares living in the northern regions of the world weigh an average of about 5kg (11lbs), those in temperate regions average about 3kg (6.5lbs) and those closest

This silver-coloured Brown hare in the Norfolk snow looks deceptively similar to the Mountain hare. However they are in fact different species

to the equator only about 2kg (4.5lbs). However this is a rough guide and does not apply to all the species for instance in North America the northern Snowshoe hare (or Snowshoe rabbit) only averages about 1.5kg (3.3lbs) while the southern Antelope jackrabbit weighs 4.5kg (over 9lbs).

Everything about hares seems to be confusing because in some countries hares are called 'rabbits' and in others animals that are called hares do not in fact belong to the family of Leporidae at all.

Pikas, distant relatives of the hare

In the USA the diminutive Northern pika (*Ochotona alpina*) which lives at high elevations from Alaska to New Mexico is sometimes called a Mouse hare, a Whistling hare or a Calling hare. This species is also found across Siberia, north-eastern China and Japan. Pika are only distant relatives of the hare but they are very interesting little creatures. They look more like a large hamster with rounded ears and despite living at such high altitudes do not hibernate but instead store food for the winter.

The Large-eared pika (*Ochotona macrotis*) is the highest living mammal in the world and can be found in the Himalayas and high altitude mountain ranges in Asia. Incredibly, it survives at altitudes in excess of 20,000 feet (6,000m).

The smallest pika is the Steppe pika (*Ochotona pusilla*) which is less than 7 inches (18cms) in length and weighs between 2.7–7.4oz (75–210gms). It lives in the steppe regions of the upper Volga river, southern Ural mountains and up to the Chinese border. Surprisingly even rabbits can live at high altitudes. The Omilteme cottontail (*Sylvilagus insonus*) can be found up to 17,300 feet (5,250m) in Sierra Madre Del Sur in Mexico.

Neither pika nor hare

The same size as a guinea pig, the 'Nelson hare' (*Romerolagus nelsoni*) found on the slopes of a Mexican volcano is not actually a hare; nor is the so-called 'Sumatran hare' which is in fact a rabbit – *Nesolagus netscheri* (see page 17).

Another hare that is not a hare is a kangaroo-like animal found in Africa called the 'Spring hare' (*Pedetes capensis*). It is a rodent and has a long tail, short fore legs and long powerful hind legs, it is about 16 inches (40cms) long and can cover at least 10 feet (3 metres) in a single hop.

As long ago as 1840 it was noted that there were four distinct species of hare in North America. They were recorded as being the American hare, the Prairie hare, the Little Big Chief hare and the Polar hare. Nowadays, in America hares are called rabbits. The jackrabbit (sometimes called Jack or Jackass rabbit), is the common name given to the native North American hare

Below
Everything is big in Texas! An early 20th century joke postcard of a Black-tailed jackrabbit

False hares

There are several species that are not true hares.

HISPID HARE (also called the BRISTLY HARE or ASSAM RABBIT)
Caprolagus hispidus
It has an unusual coarse bristly coat, short broad ears and stout legs. It digs burrows and is found in the forest and grassy bamboo thickets of Nepal, Assam and north-east India. Length about 46cm (18in) Endangered species.

BUSHMAN HARE or RIVERINE RABBIT
Bunolagus monticularis
Inhabits the Cape Province and eastern South Africa. Endangered species.

NATAL RED HARE, also called the GREATER RED ROCK HARE
Pronolagus crassicaudatus
This genus are called 'rock jumpers'. They have shorter legs and are of stouter build than most species of hare, inhabiting stony ground in Botswana, Zimbabwe, Namibia and South Africa. Length: 46cm (18in).
Other 'Rock hares' are: Jameson's Red rock hare (*Pronolagus randensis*) and Smith's Red roch hare (*Pronolagus rupestris*)

NELSON HARE *Romerolagus nelsoni*
This is a guinea pig-sized rock hare found on the slopes of a Mexican volcano.

SUMATRAN HARE *Nesolagus netscheri*
A rabbit which lives in rocky habitats.

In North America rabbits are known as cottontails *(above)* but the hare, confusingly, is called a jackrabbit

which can leap up to 20 feet (6m) and reach speeds up to 45 miles (70km) an hour. Jackrabbits are one of the most social groups of hares. In the USA most rabbits are called 'cottontails'.

The domesticated 'Belgian hare' is also a giant rabbit.

The True Hares of North and South America

BLACK-TAILED JACKRABBIT *Lepus californicus*

The tail is black and it has black-tipped ears which are up to 8 inches (20cm) long. Its weight is about 8lbs (3.5kg) and it inhabits the grassland, steppe and semi-desert areas of central and south-western North America, northern Mexico and Baja California where it feeds on mesquite scrub as well as on grass. Black-tailed jackrabbits have been recorded as travelling on ten-mile round trips to feed on alfalfa fields. They are social animals and large groups of 25 or more will sometimes congregate. The Black-tailed jackrabbit has been introduced to some of the eastern states of the USA and to Nantucket Island.

ANTELOPE JACKRABBIT *Lepus alleni*

Related to the Black-tailed jackrabbit, the Antelope jackrabbit has even larger ears which have no black on the tips It is a lighter colour on its sides and rump and these appear to flash as it leaps. Weighing 9-10lbs (4.5kg) it inhabits the steppe and desert areas of southern Arizona, north-western Mexico and Tiburon Island in the Gulf of California.

The Black-tailed Jackrabbit (*Lepus californicus*). There are four species of hare in North America that are called jackrabbits. The Black-tailed jackrabbit (*below*) inhabits the grassland, steppe and semi-desert areas of central and south-western North America, Baja California and northern Mexico (*photo courtesy of D. Kjaer*)

BLACK JACKRABBIT *Lepus insularis*
This hare inhabits Espiritu Santo Island off south-eastern Baja California. Endangered species.

SAGE HARE *Lepus syvaticus nuttalli*
The Sage hare inhabits the arid regions of western North America. Recently, some naturalists have suggested that it might in fact be a variety of the common Cottontail or Wood rabbit. So its current status as a hare is unclear. It been recorded as far south as New Mexico.

WHITE-SIDED JACKRABBIT or MEXICAN HARE
Lepus callotis mexicanus
It inhabits high grassland regions of north-western and central Mexico and south-western New Mexico. Unusually for hares, this species form a strong pair bond and averages three litters of two young each year. It is a species that is officially at risk.

TEHUANTEPEC JACKRABBIT *Lepus flavigularis*
This endangered species inhabits extreme southern Mexico.

WHITE-TAILED JACKRABBIT *Lepus townsendii*
Another large jackrabbit, the white-tailed one measures about 20 inches (50cm) in length and weighs about 7lbs (3.2 kg). It inhabits the colder grassland and steppe areas of the north-western states of America. The tail is white all year and the coat usually turns a paler colour in winter, sometimes turning completely white.

Above
The Snowshoe hare, known in the USA as the Snowshoe rabbit, got its name from its large hind feet which help it to move around on the snow in the mountains of North America
(photo courtesy Allan Hales)

SNOWSHOE HARE *Lepus americanus*
It is also sometimes called the Varying hare because it is dark brown in summer and usually turns white in winter but keeps the black tips on its ears. It inhabits the far northern mountainous and open forest areas of Canada and North America from Alaska to Newfoundland where it was introduced in the 1860s and consequently displaced the indigenous Arctic hare from most regions below the tree line.

Once the most important small game animal in Canada, and a vital source of meat for the fur trappers, homesteaders and Indians, the Snowshoe hare (widely known in North America as the Snowshoe rabbit) is now found as far south as the mountains of central California and northern New Mexico.

It acquired the name of Snowshoe hare because it has large wide furry paws that give it a good footing on ice and loose snow. Its length is 13–20inches (32–50cms) and average weight 3.3–4.4lbs (1.5–2kg). The Snowshoe hare undergoes remarkable fluctuations in numbers that peak every 8–11 years. During this period, the population may differ one hundred fold. The peaks and troughs are believed to be caused by a complex link between the Snowshoe hare and the lynx that preys on it.

ALASKAN or TUNDRA HARE *Lepus othus*

It is found in the west and south west of Alaska and the extreme eastern tip of Siberia. It is said to be the largest lagomorph with an average weight of nearly 10.5 lbs (5kg) and a length of 20–24 inches (51-61cm).

ARCTIC HARE *Lepus timidus var. Lepus arcticus*

The Arctic hare is found in the tundra zone of Canada, Greenland and Newfoundland. It is a sub-species of the European Arctic/Mountain hare. It turns white in winter and the average weight is 8.5–11 lb (4–5kg). Arctic hares feed on woody plants, mosses, lichens and berries. Most unusually for hares, they are reported to be fond of meat such as young voles and are attracted to meat used to bait traps set to catch foxes. Sometimes they are caught in them. Breeding takes place only in summer when one, occasionally two litters of four to eight young are

Left
The Arctic hare, unusual for for its carnivorous tendencies: it will eat young voles and other small mammals in order to supplement its diet

The Arctic hare
(*Lepus arcticus*) in the process
of changing its coat.
It is a sub-species of *Lepus
timidus* (the Mountain hare)
which also turns white in winter.
The Arctic hare inhabits the
tundra zone of Canada,
Greenland and Newfoundland

produced. Adults sometimes form groups of up to 300 animals. The Alaskan hare, the Mountain hare (of Europe and Asia) and the Arctic hare are genetically indistinguishable.

The True Hares of the African Continent

ETHIOPIAN HIGHLAND HARE *Lepus starcki*
The Ethiopian Highland hare inhabits the mountains of central Ethiopia. It has very long ears and legs and is an endangered species.

ETHIOPIAN HARE *Lepus fagani*

It inhabits scrubland in western Ethiopia and the adjacent parts of Sudan and Kenya.

ABYSSINIAN HARE *Lepus habessinicus*

Inhabits eastern Ethiopia and Somalia.

SCRUB HARE *Lepus saxatilis*

The Scrub hare is distinguishable from other African hares by its large size and long ears. It inhabits mountainous regions in southern Namibia and western and southern South Africa.

AFRICAN SAVANNA HARE *Lepus victoriae*

It inhabits Senegal, southern Sudan, northern Namibia and south and eastern areas of South Africa.

CRAWSHAY'S HARE *Lepus victoriae crawshayi*

Found in the Transvaal, Somalia and Senegal it is closely related to the Indian hare. Another near-identical hare is *Lepus victoriae whytei* (Malawi hare) which inhabits parts of East Africa and is similar to Crawshay's and the African Savanna hare.

CAPE HARE *Lepus capensis*

The name *Lepus capensis* was first applied to a hare from the Cape of Good Hope in 1758. *Capensis* is the most abundant of all species of hares and it is widespread across the non-forested parts of Africa, southern Europe, the Middle East, central Asia and eastern China. It is thought to be very closely related to the Brown hare. 80 sub-species have been recorded.

Cape hares are highly adaptable and can thrive in grassland, steppe and desert habitats, even where it has been over-grazed. Sub-species can be found at sea level, as well as in the Gobi desert and alpine meadows up to 15,000 feet (3,000m).

They vary greatly in size and appearance, with weights ranging from 2.2–8lbs (1–3.5kg) and vary in colour from a pale sandy buff to a rusty brown on their backs. They are usually white underneath.

It is likely that the species of hare which inhabits Sardinia (*Lepus capensis mediterraneus*) is a sub-species of the Cape hare.

Above
The head and large ears of a Cape hare can just be seen as they disappear down the throat of a Kenyan cheetah. It was a chase witnessed, and captured at the end on camera, by David Mason

The Granada hare (*Lepus capensis granatens*), found in Spain, and the Tolai hare (*Lepus capensis tolai*), found in Mongolia, Kazakhstan, Russia and Beijing are two further sub-species.

Arabian Cape hares

There are six species of Cape hare living on mainland Arabia which have exceptionally long ears and whose coat colour varies to match the local terrain. Two more species live on off-shore Arabian islands that are smaller and have shorter ears. These are the Masirah hare (*Lepus capensis jefferyi*) which lives on Masirah Island and Sana Atallah's hare (*Lepus capensis atallahi*) found on Bahrain Island.

The largest of the hares in mainland Arabia is *Lepus capensis syriacus* which is found in Syria, Lebanon and northern Israel. Local arabic names for the hares in Arabia are Arnab, Arneeb, Harneeb and Haineeb. Three species live in the United Arab Emirates and are collectively known as Arabian or Desert hares. They are respectively: the Sand hare (*Lepus capensis cheesmani*), the Arabian hare (*Lepus capensis arabicus*) and the Omani hare (*Lepus capensis omanensis*) – which is very small with proportionally enormous ears and it inhabits the mountains of the UAE, as well as Oman.

Above
This Arabian hare has a pale, almost bleached, coat which gives it the perfect camouflage for its life among the sands of Dubai
(*photo courtesy of Declan O'Donovan*)

Desert survival

Desert conditions here are extreme and hares that live in this inhospitable environment have to be able to withstand day-time temperatures soaring to above 50C and dropping to only a little above freezing at night. They rely on succulent plants for their water intake as typically rain only falls on ten days each year.

Desert hares are only about one third the size of a Brown hare and they can run at speeds up to 45mph (70km per hour). They do not pant or sweat and avoid water loss by excreting dry faeces and concentrated urine. Increased blood flow to their large ears helps to cool them. They also have a lower metabolic rate than the Brown hare.

Desert hares breed all year round but only have one or two babies at a time after a gestation period of 42 days.

They have traditionally been an important food source for

Bedouin tribes who either caught them where they were resting or hunted them with falcons and saluki dogs. The Arabian hare in several Middle Eastern countries was nearly hunted to extinction with firearms. Consequently, hunting them in Abu Dhabi Emirate and the United Arab Emirates has been prohibited as direct result of concern over declining hare populations.

Falconry has always been a popular traditional sport in the Arabian Gulf and the empty Quarter of Saudi Arabia still offers Arab falconers the opportunity to fly their Saker falcons, the best breed for hunting the small desert hare.

The True Hares of Asia

JAPANESE HARE *Lepus brachyurus*
The Japanese hare inhabits Honshu, Shikoku, Kyushu, Sado, and Oki islands (Japan.) It turns white in winter.

MANCHURIAN HARE *Lepus mandschuricus*
The forests of Manchuria, North Korea and the lower Amur region of south-eastern Siberia are home to the Manchurian hare.

KOREAN HARE *Lepus coreanus*
Inhabits Korea and southern Manchuria.

MANCHURIAN BLACK HARE *Lepus melainus*
Inhabits Manchuria. Endangered species.

CHINESE HARE *Lepus sinensis*
Inhabits eastern China, northern Vietnam and Taiwan.

YARKAND HARE *Lepus yarkandensis*
Inhabits southern Sinkiang (China) and is a species at risk.

HAINAN HARE *Lepus hainanus*
Inhabits Hainan Island off southern China. Endangered species.

YUNNAN HARE *Lepus comus*
Inhabits Yunnan and western Guizhou provinces of south-central China.

BURMESE HARE *Lepus peguensis*
Inhabits Burma, Thailand and Indo-china.

WOOLLY HARE *Lepus oiostolus*
The Woolly hare lives at higher altitudes than any other hare. One reliable report records a sighting at 19,800ft (6,053m) but its normal range is between 8,200ft (2,560m) and 17,700ft (5,400m). It is found in the mountains of Tibet and adjacent highlands of China, Nepal and Kashmir.

INDIAN HARE *Lepus nigricollis*
Inhabits Pakistan, India, Bangladesh, Nepal, Sikkim, Bhutan, Sri Lanka and has been introduced to Java.

Hares in Australia and New Zealand

There are no indigenous species of hare in Australia and New Zealand, but introductions have been here made of the Brown hare and the Cape hare. In Australia an animal called a hare-wallaby (*Lagorchestes leporides*) filled the niche occupied by hares in other countries but has now become very rare.

The Brown hare was imported to New Zealand and naturalised by European settlers in the 1870s where it is now hunted on horseback by 27 packs of hounds across the country. The first hunt was formed at Pakuranga, near Auckland, in 1873 and is still in existence.

Australia and New Zealand have no indigenous species of hare, but the Brown hare was introduced to both countries by the white settlers in the 1800s

The True Hares of Europe

BROOM HARE *Lepus castrovieoi*
The Broom hare inhabits the Cantabrian Mountains of north-western Spain. In appearance it closely resembles the Brown hare and weighs about 6lbs (2.7kg). It is a species at risk.

BROWN HARE *Lepus europaeus*

The Brown hare inhabits southern Scandinavia, northern Spain, and is spread across Europe to western Siberia, China and north-western Iran. It is found in lowland Britain and some parts of Northern Ireland and has been introduced to Argentina, Chile, Uruguay, Australia, New Zealand, the Falkland Islands and the Great Lakes area of north-eastern USA, and south-eastern Canada where it was originally released in Ontario and is sometimes known there as the Cape hare. In 1976, the Brown hare was reported to be of economic importance in Poland with hunters killing about 700,000 annually out of an estimated population of 3.2 million.

MOUNTAIN or BLUE HARE *Lepus timidus*
The Mountain hare inhabits tundra and open forests in northern Eurasia, the Alps, Central Asia and parts of Japan. In Britain it is found on high ground in Scotland and north Derbyshire. The Irish hare is a sub-species of the Mountain hare.

The Hares of Britain and Ireland

BROWN HARE *Lepus europaeus*
The Brown hare is also known as the European hare. Confusingly, in the 19th century, it was sometimes referred to as *Lepus timidus*.

It is a tawny brown on its back with white under-parts and black-tipped ears. The top side of the tail is also black. Its length is 24–28ins (60–70cm) and average weight is about 8–10lbs

Below right
Mountain hares are also called 'Varying' or 'Variable' hares because their coats change from white to brown in Spring and vice versa in the autumn. This one was photographed in March

Below left
The Scottish Mountain hare (*Lepus timidus scoticus*) in summer coat.
Mountain hares are distributed throughout colder regions of the Northern Hemisphere. In Britain it is found only at elevations above c.1500ft (500m) in Scotland, the Isle of Man and Derbyshire

(4–4.7kg). A Brown hare shot at Welford in Northamptonshire weighed 15lb 1oz. Brown hares have been introduced to many of the islands off the British coast and to north-west Ireland. In England, Wales and Scotland they are found up to an elevation of about 1,500 feet (500m) normally in open country, farmland and on chalk downlands.

MOUNTAIN or BLUE or WHITE HARE
Lepus timidus scoticus
Also sometimes called the Scottish, Alpine, Varying or Variable hare. In the 19th century it was occasionally referred to as the Arctic hare (*Lepus variabilis*)

The summer coat is blue/brown, white in winter and shaded in spring and autumn when the coat is changing. It has an all-white tail and black tipped ears that are much shorter than those of the Brown hare. Average length is about 20 inches (50cm) and average weight 5.5–6.6lbs (2.5–3kg) but in good habitat a proportion of Mountain hares may exceed 7lb (3.25kg).

Above
When the Brown hare, *Lepus europeaus*, was introduced to Britain, the indigenous Mountain hare was probaly forced to live at higher elevations

IRISH HARE *Lepus timidus hibernicus*
The Irish hare is one of Ireland's longest established mammals. It is a sub-species of the Mountain hare but is thought to be genetically distinct from the Scottish Mountain hare and more closely related to those found on the European mainland. It was formerly recognised as a species in 1833 but the oldest dated specimen is reported to be 28,000 years old.

The Irish hare is a russet colour in summer, sometimes lighter in winter, and very occasionally with white patches. The underparts are white, as is the whole of its tail. Its average length is 21 ins (55cm) and average weight is about 7.7lbs (3.5kg). It can run at speeds up to 30mph (48kph). Breeding takes place between December and October and litters average 2 or 3 young. Maximum life expectation is around nine years.

The Irish hare is seldom seen during the daytime unless flushed and it appears to be generally more placid by nature than the Brown hare.

It occurs naturally all over Ireland in a wide range of habitats at all altitudes but, like the Brown hare, numbers have

Below
The white coat of the Mountain hare looks highly conspicuous after the snows have melted

been declining in many areas. While still quite common in the west of Ireland where it will spend the day hidden in cover on the rough hillsides, it tends to venture out to feed on the improved grassland of the lower in-bye fields at dusk.

In the east of Ireland, however, it has become quite a rarity. As elsewhere, this is likely to be due to the changes in farming in the 1960s and 1970s: new pastoral management including a great increase in silage-making, extensive use of chemicals, the tidying of rough areas and fewer varieties of native grasses in pastures. Researchers from Queen's University, Belfast, have fitted radio-collars to a number of Irish hares and are conducting DNA tests in an effort to unravel some of the mysteries surrounding its life. Although not strictly endangered, complete protection was given, controversially, to the Irish hare in Northern Ireland for one year as from January 2004.

It is interesting that both the Mountain hare and Brown hare are found on the Isle of Man which is only 13.5 miles wide and 32.5 miles long. Brown hares are said to be native there and

The Irish hare is very adaptable and lives in areas of mixed farming, grassland, moorland, mountains and dry peat bogs

Left
The Irish hare (*Lepus timidus hibernicus*) is widespread across Ireland but in decline and scarce in some areas. This sub-species of the mountain hare has adapted to living in a variety of habitats in Ireland. It does not turn white in winter and can be differentiated from the Brown hare by its shorter ears and entirely white tail

are found throughout the island, abundantly in some places. The Mountain hare is believed to have been introduced a century or so ago. They are limited in their distribution to the northern hills only but numbers are good in the areas they do frequent. It has also been suggested that Irish hares at one time were introduced but there is no evidence of this now. It is worth remembering that there are no foxes on the Isle of Man.

Natural History of the
Hare in Britain & Ireland

Both hares and rabbits belong to the order of mammals known as Lagomorphs. They may look alike, but that is where the similarity ends, for they behave in completely different ways.

Most species of hare are larger in size than a rabbit and have a more angular less rounded body and longer ears and legs. The colour of the coat is usually a shade of brown with a white under-belly and the eyes are prominent, allowing for all-round vision. The black tipped ears, like those of a horse, can be moved independently to pick up sounds. Hares have strong hind legs and furry feet with sharp claws which they use to great effect if they are captured.

There have always been unexplained fluctuations in the population of different species of hares. Records of Brown hares on one estate in England, close to the Norfolk/Suffolk border, clearly showed this phenomenon over the first half of the last century. Between 1901 and 1950, numbers in the game book varied from just over 1,000 in some years to a peak of 3,000 in

Brown hares boxing. This interaction between 'mad March hares' is usually the result of a doe fending off the unwanted attentions of a potential suitor

the 1913/14 season. A century ago it is thought there were four times as many Brown hares as there is now. They could even be found within the City of London.

From the early 1940s there was a significant drop in hare numbers, partly due to the fact that during the Second World War there was little predator control: most gamekeepers were away fighting for their country and hares were probably also shot or snared for food during this time of shortage.

During the course of the war, it is likely that the population in some areas was reduced to such a low level that it was unable to fully recover. However available statistics indicate that hare numbers have stabilised during the last ten years, albeit at a low level in some places.

It has been observed on many sporting estates that 2003 was a good year for Brown hares, thought most likely to have been due to kind weather during the spring and summer.

Right
A wash and a brush up for a Brown hare as it makes use of a gamekeeper's cover crop of maize

Below
Although the hare usually likes open spaces it is not unusual to find a Brown hare in woodland

The British Brown Hare
Lepus europaeus

The Brown hare is thought to have moved eastwards from the steppes of Asia, as man cleared the forests for farming during the Neolithic period. One theory put forward is that they arrived in Britain when it was still joined to Europe by a land bridge, before sea levels rose. An opposing theory is that they were introduced to Britain by the Romans in the 1st century AD. A third theory put forward makes both the other two plausible: that they died out during the last Ice Age and were re-introduced by the Romans. Fossil evidence shows that Brown hares were certainly present in Britain two thousand years ago. They were also

Left
A Brown hare in an open stubble field needs to be vigilant

38

mentioned in the Domesday-book as being observed on the hillside above the village of Stockton in Wiltshire.

As the art of growing crops developed, so did the territorial range of the Brown hare. Mountain hares are indigenous to Britain and the arrival of the Brown hare with its larger size and preference for low ground probably forced the Mountain hare to adapt to living at a higher elevation.

Hares are mysterious creatures and seem to have split personalities – the Jekyll and Hydes of the animal world. Generally secretive, retiring and giving the impression of being timid, they can at times be bold, reckless and even pugnacious. They can appear to be both clever and stupid at the same time.

For centuries the Brown hare had been highly valued for the sport it offered and consequently was protected. Prior to 1840 it is known that they were sometimes even kept in small warrens from which they could be caught up in traps or nets so that they could be used for hunting or coursing. These 'released' hares would usually run in a straight line because they were unfamiliar with the area in which they were freed.

A Brown hare in her form. Her camouflage is not so effective when there is snow on the ground

Fluctuations in Brown hare populations

Brown hare numbers peaked in the 19th century. In *Rural Rides* by William Cobbett, published in 1830, he described seeing "an acre of hares" on Salisbury Plain in the October of 1822. On being disturbed they had gathered together like a flock of sheep. It is thought the population of Brown hares at this time was about 4 million.

A dramatic decline in Brown hare numbers occurred at the end of the 19th century. In 1880 the *Ground Game Act* permitted tenants to kill the hares on their land. It is interesting to note that in Baily's *Magazine of Sports and Pastimes* May 1906, a Mr Alan R. Haig Brown wrote an article deploring the inadequacies of the *Ground Game Act* in not providing hares with a close season.

Even a hundred years ago he commented on the fact that

Dry Tastes

Hares do not flourish in the wetter areas of Britain. They thrive best on light, dry land such as covers parts of Yorkshire, East Anglia, Berkshire, Oxfordshire, Wiltshire and Gloucestershire

Hares are caught up and re-located for many different reasons. This three compartment hare box is probably a hundred years old. This is a safe way for hares to be transported

certain regions including Norfolk had enormous populations of Brown hares, 'yet other localities of England are so denuded of hares that the creatures demand almost as much protection as would a pair of Golden Eagles in Hyde Park'. Legally, there still isn't a close season for hares although those who course, hunt and shoot for sport operate a voluntary one.

All through the last century, Brown hare numbers have continued to decline for a variety of reasons, mostly related to agricultural practices. There was a slight recovery in the Brown hare population in the late 1950s possibly because of the huge reduction in rabbit numbers following the spread of myxomatosis. It was also a time when bird of prey numbers were at an all-time low. Since the early 1960s, modern farming methods have accounted for more deaths and loss of habitat.

Reasons for post-war decline

It has been estimated that in the 30 years after World War II, the hare population fell by 75%. Interestingly the number of lapwings who share the same habitat as hares also fell correspondingly. Intensive farming, the increasing use of toxic chemicals on the land, removal of sheltering hedges, general loss of habitat, over-shooting combined with a series of cold wet springs all affected numbers. The practice of burning unwanted straw in the fields after harvest no doubt accounted for quite a

number of deaths, especially where it was policy to light the straw around the perimeter and burn the field inwards. There was no escape for hares when they were surrounded by flames. Thankfully this practice ceased in the early 1980s.

The popularity of making silage in preference to hay, brought about by the new convenient method of storing it in plastic bags, has also added to the decline in hare numbers. Hares and their leverets often hide in grass fields and are cut up when the grass is mowed. This can now happen two or three times a year for silage production, whereas there was only one cut made for hay.

The Brown hare found in Britain is generally shy, timid and highly-strung by nature; so much so that it has been known to die of fright. But paradoxically they can occasionally be found living in close proximity to man, in places such as golf courses. Here there may be patches of thick cover such as gorse where they can hide during the daytime and good food is easily accessible after dark on the undisturbed greens.

Distribution of the Brown hare

Hares do not like to live in the wetter areas of Britain and they thrive best on light dry land such as that in parts of Yorkshire, East Anglia, Berkshire, Oxfordshire, Wiltshire and Gloucestershire. In these areas Brown hares can be present in such numbers as to make culling a necessity. On the arable chalk downlands of Hampshire hares are quite plentiful in some places but there are fewer in neighbouring Sussex. There is more pressure on hares in the open grassland of the Downs, in which many areas close to large urban populations are opened up for human recreation and therefore become prone to a considerable amount of disturbance.

Open farmland and downland at levels below 1,500 feet (500 metres) is the favoured habitat of the Brown hare, particularly farms where barley, wheat, sugar beet and fallow land in the form of late stubble and set-aside are available. 60% of the British Brown hare population is to be found in arable areas, about 24% on pastoral land, 11% on marginal uplands and only 5% in the uplands. The latter range may overlap with that of the

Opposite
Hopefully the new agro-environmental schemes included in the EU Bio-diversity Action Plan (BAP) will help increase the number of Brown hares across Britain

Brown hare in Ireland

Several attempts have been made in the past to introduce the Brown hare to Ireland but only a small population has survived – all in Northern Ireland

Above
The Brown hare: shy, timid and highly-strung

Mountain hare. More than 20% of the total Brown hare population is to be found in East Anglia. Grasslands grazed by sheep are not usually good habitats for hares as the sheep nibble the grass close to the ground, reducing the hare's cover and food.

Cattle are more beneficial to hares because they graze inefficiently and leave many tussocks of grass in which leverets can hide. On the negative side of cattle farming, fields of lush grass are usually left for silage. These are also attractive to leverets but unfortunately the machinery used to cut the grass can be lethal for them.

Young hares are also at risk from predation, especially by foxes, and benefit greatly from the protection afforded them by gamekeepers. The shelter provided by game crops planted for shooting interests is also advantageous to hares.

Few Brown hares are found in Wales and the West Country and none in north-west Scotland or the western Highlands, although some of the Scottish Islands have maintained small populations after the Brown hare was introduced there. Several attempts have also been made in the past to introduce them to Ireland but only a few have survived in Northern Ireland.

Above
Brown hares shed their winter coats in Spring

Below
Brown hare leverets are weaned by the time they are 4-6 weeks old

Colour variations in Brown hares is not uncommon but this Norfolk hare with a white face is very unusual. Brown hares can run up to a speed of 45mph (70kms) and often zig-zag or turn at right angles when chased, to elude being caught

Survival rates

It is estimated that Brown hares in Britain survive for an average of three to four years on arable land but have a shorter life expectancy on land entirely laid down to improved grassland. The poet Cowper, who kept some tame hares, had one that lived for nearly nine years and another until it was twelve.

Reproduction and therefore population rates on grassland are obviously affected by the shorter life expectancy as well as the fact that the bodily condition of the hares is generally poorer in these areas. This in itself results in the hares being more susceptible to predation, disease and bad weather conditions. Although hares are prolific and can produce up to ten young in a good year, there can be quite a large variation from year to year in the numbers produced.

The young are born on top of ground and rely on camouflage to conceal them in vegetation. Adult hares also rely on camouflage but have the benefit of speed and stamina should they need to flee.

The hare in flight

A hare's first line of defence when it spots danger is to lie low: to press itself down close to the ground in its form, only taking flight when it is under imminent threat. Brown hares can run up to a speed of 45mph (70kms) and often zig-zag or turn at right angles when chased, to elude being caught. The action of a greyhound in full flight exactly mirrors that of a hare. The long hind legs are thrust forward and the fore legs backwards

Tell tale sign

When it is disturbed a hare runs away with its tail held downwards showing the black colouration on the upper surface

between them. When not in danger, a hare will casually rise and stretch before lolloping off and stopping to sit up every now and then to look around especially if it has passed through a hedge. Because of their build, chased hares usually choose to run uphill, which gives them an advantage over other animals. All hares possess larger hearts and a bigger volume of blood within their bodies than animals of comparable size; this gives them greater speed, endurance and stamina.

Although hares don't hold territories as such, Brown hares will soon return to their home ground once the danger which caused them to flee has passed.

The hare's coat

There is some variation in the colour of the coat of a Brown hare. It is usually a tawny colour with a white underbelly and is soft and dense. In winter, the hare has a layer of guard hairs. A few white Brown hares can be found in Dorset, but black coloured ones are very rare. In February 1828, a black hare was shot near Coventry and another was killed at Netley in Shropshire. Pied Brown hares or those flecked with white are sometimes seen. Moulting takes place in spring and autumn.

The hair from a hare's ear is often used for tying artificial flies used by fly fishermen. Dried hare's ears can be bought in pairs and the fur on the backs of them removed and twisted on to waxed cotton (known as dubbing) to form the body part of fishing flies, such as the popular Hare's Ear Nymph.

Unlike a rabbit, when it is disturbed a hare runs away with

Above
Brown hare in a field of young barley showing off her white belly as she relaxes in the sunshine.
Male hares are usually slightly smaller and lighter than females, but apart from that, the sexes are almost identical in appearance

Above
A relaxed, unthreatened hare will usually stretch when it gets up from the form

The action of a greyhound in full flight exactly mirrors that of a hare. The long hind legs are thrust forward and the fore legs backwards between them

its tail held downwards showing the black colouration on the upper surface. A rabbit when it runs carries its tail upright showing the white underside which acts as an alarm signal. It is generally agreed that rabbits and hares do not mix. Rabbits are gregarious, nibble the vegetation very short and can be quite aggressive even to hares. Hares therefore are found in different habitats to those chosen by rabbits.

Hare behaviour

Hares are mostly solitary by nature although there are times when they form social or family groups or gather where there is food that is particularly to their liking.

The 'boxing' hares in spring that gave rise to the term 'Mad as a March Hare' is not, as was previously thought, males fighting but a doe attempting to ward off the unwanted and over-zealous attentions of the jacks (males). There have also been sightings of hares whirling round standing upright on their hind legs, holding their ears down for no apparent reason. If confined in close proximity, hares will attack each other.

Not, as the casual observer might surmise, two male hares fighting: boxing takes place between a doe and a jack during courtship

While hares are not strictly territorial, they do tend to stay within an area and have 'ranges'. Does tend to be more static than the males, although a male hare will travel a long distance to seek out females on heat. Bucks are promiscuous and their energetic chasing, scratching, biting and boxing antics are very obvious in the springtime and certainly attract attention. In the spring, several hares can often be seen hopping, apparently aimlessly, around a field sometimes in procession.

Hares are mainly nocturnal, and because they are so active when darkness falls, they have become associated with evil and mystery. Come sun up, they seem to mysteriously disappear. A field where only one or two may be spotted during daylight may well have a dozen or twenty in after dark.

The form

Brown hares do not live in burrows. Instead, during the daytime they nestle in the vegetation or scratch out a shallow indentation in the open ground, called a form in which they crouch down with their ears flattened against their back and become almost invisible. Rough ploughed or cultivated ground is a natural choice for hiding in. These 'forms' may be used on a regular basis and can become worn smooth.

They are approached by the hare with great care in order to baffle the scent trail, by using a devious route, back-tracking and leaping. It is said that a Brown hare can leap up to 18 feet and one has been recorded clearing one of the Grand National fences! In these forms, mostly sheltered from the wind, hares will sit out in even the worst of weather. In summer, they choose to spend the day couched in a form in the shade and in winter they seek the warmth of the sun. The form will always be in a

Above
Hares grooming themselves. Like all wild creatures they need to keep themselves clean. While normally solitary, in springtime hares can sometimes be seen in groups like this

Secret of the hare's stamina

All hares possess larger hearts and a bigger volume of blood within their bodies than animals of comparable size. This gives them greater speed, endurance and stamina

place that affords them a good view.

One 19th century writer could not imagine a 'more cheerless wretched existence' than living out in open fields. He thought hares must be 'at great risk of getting stiff with rheumatism.' He could however understand that they might not want to live in woods in autumn as 'the noise of falling leaves would keep them in a constant state of alarm.'

Hare's vision

Brown hares have large golden-coloured eyes set on the side of their heads, providing them with almost 360 degree vision. Directly ahead of them is where they can see least. They have been known to kill themselves by running into an object or even each other because they have obviously been looking backwards at whatever was behind them rather than forward. This all-round vision means that from their hiding place they can view everything about them. It is a fallacy that hares never

One 19th century writer could not imagine a 'more cheerless wretched existence' than living out in open fields

close their eyes. They shut them when they are fighting to avoid injury and also when they are dozing. In common with many other animals that are the prey rather than the hunter, they do not go into a deep sleep, as we do. They probably merely relax and cat nap.

Hare routes

Hares are creatures of habit and use the same tracks and gaps in hedges, which has always made them easy for poachers with nets or snares. They also make good use of the unsown lines left in arable crops which are now such a part of modern farming practices. When they are chased they know exactly where they are heading.

Senses of the hare

Hares have good scenting abilities and excellent hearing. They are not very vocal apart from emitting an exceedingly loud, blood-curdling scream when they are attacked. However, quiet grunts, snuffles and teeth-grinding have been noted and a doe runs around snorting if fighting to protect her young.

Hares are very sensitive to weather changes. In windy conditions they are wary when feeding. Their hearing is finely tuned and no doubt this tool of survival is impaired when the wind is blowing strongly.

It is therefore an odd fact that in the past Brown hares have made their homes on many airfields including major ones such as Gatwick. Perhaps it is more than coincidence that a hare will unnecessarily run alongside or in front of a vehicle for a quarter of a mile or more before veering off. In fact hares often give the impression that they enjoy the chance to show off their paces or play the game of 'chicken'. Maybe they like to race, or some suggest it is the vibrations and noise from machines that incite this behaviour.

Tame ones have been known to get pleasure from drumming on an empty box or other container with their front paws, even for quite long periods. They are also said to show signs of actually enjoying the noise and atmosphere of a violent

Swimming hares

There are many accounts of hares swimming voluntarily or when they are hard pressed by dogs. Distances of up to a mile across water, the sea included, have been recorded

Right
Hares can move their ears individually backwards and forwards

thunderstorm. William Cowper in his poem *Epitaph on a Hare* noted his tame hare Tiney became active in the evenings and mostly 'before approaching showers or when a storm drew near.' Hares certainly seem fascinated by loud noises and perhaps this is another reason why they have become associated with darkness and evil in the past.

Refection

In common with rabbits, hares are known to eat their own droppings. This habit is called 'refection'. A soft form of faeces is passed first which the hare consumes; thus the food it eats passes through its digestive system twice. After this has happened, the droppings passed the second time are drier and more fibrous. This process of refection is necessary for the hare's well being.

Below
A pair of Brown hares in set-aside. Although a creature of the open countryside, Brown hares can also be found sheltering on the edge of woodland during the daytime, concealed against the base of a tree, especially in bad weather

Grooming

Like all wild creatures, it is important for a hare to keep itself clean and they are always grooming. This puts them at risk of ingesting chemicals sprayed on the land, especially because they like to keep their feet clean after being balled up with mud. The risk of chemical poisoning to hares has decreased, as pesticides are used more sparingly and are a lot safer, but paraquat is still often sprayed on stubble after the harvest to kill off any growth, and this can be harmful to hares.

A hare's feet are covered in fur which give it an advantage when running uphill in snow or on slippery ground. It will usually choose to use this advantage when being pursued

Relocating hares

Sometimes it is necessary to relocate live hares for restocking. This may be carried out for many reasons, including conservation, coursing, hunting, shooting or just to introduce some fresh blood. Because they are creatures of habit using regular paths, gateways or gaps through hedges, hares required for relocation are usually caught by driving them into nets placed across their pathways. They become entangled in them and can then be quickly caught by hand. Occasionally, individuals can be netted at night by using a spotlight to dazzle them. Despite being highly strung, once confined individually in the darkness of carrying boxes, they can be safely moved long distances.

The Mountain or Blue Hare
Lepus timidus

Mountain or Blue hares have inhabited Britain for at least 12,000 years. They are often referred to as White hares.

It was reported that an effort was made to eradicate them from the Highlands of Scotland in 1919 just after World War I but this plan obviously failed because in 1930 they were said to be present in their millions. Even allowing for a large amount of exaggeration, they must still have been fairly plentiful because it was not unusual for a hare shooting party to bag 1,000 in a day and in the Cairngorms as many as 1,200.

Even today, they are still numerous in some areas, although in others there has been a sharp decrease in numbers. Some of this decline is due to the fact that not all estates, especially those with forestry interests, welcome the presence of hares.

On other estates which are managed for grouse and where Mountain hares gain from predator control and improved habitat, it is often necessary to cull them and bags of 300 or 400 are not unusual for the annual hare shoot. Mountain hares can play host to ticks that may spread disease between the sheep and grouse they share the hills and heather with.

The estimated population of Mountain hare at present is 300,000 and they are found principally in Scotland where they share their habitat with grouse and ptarmigan. They have also been introduced to some of the Scottish islands. Generally they have similar habits to the Brown hare although sometimes they gather in large groups.

The Mountain hare utilises the land that the Brown hare shuns, preferring open mountain and moorland. They tend to only be found at elevations above about 1,500ft (500 metres).

An estimated one thousand at present inhabit the Peak District in Derbyshire, where they were originally introduced in the late 1800s and early 1900s. Mountain hares can also be found on the Isle of Man. There are none elsewhere either in Wales or England.

Opposite
The Mountain/Blue hare thrives on the mountains and moorland of Scotland which are managed for grouse shooting. The varying stages of heather growth in the background result from controlled burning as part of moor management and provide the necessary cover and good quality food required by Mountain hares if they are to breed successfully

Tragedy of white hares on the Fells

An elderly retired farmer in the Lake District recalls a very severe winter when he was a boy (before World War II) when the White hares came down off the Fells to search for food in the in-bye fields. The snow was so deep that they all starved and he has never seen any white hares on the Fells since. His account that they were once established in Cumbria is backed up by the words of an old hunting song that refers to watching White hares on the Fells

Change of coat

The Mountain hare is said to moult three times each year, changing its coat from white to brown in the spring. This is a gradual process and the coat often takes on a blue tinge when this is happening. In the 19th century there was a theory that Mountain hares didn't actually moult but that the colour change was brought about by a change in the fluid that coloured the hair.

In summer the coat becomes a blue-brown colour. At this stage and with its smaller size and shorter ears than the Brown hare, it is quite similar to a rabbit in appearance. The Mountain hare is said to change its brown coat for another one in late summer, before reverting to white for the winter.

This colour change is obviously advantageous in summer and winter, but spring and autumn can be dangerous times if the animal is still brown when snow falls, or is still white when the snow melts. Mountain hares are extremely vulnerable at this time, their white coats making them conspicuous against the darkness of the heather. Likewise, an unseasonable fall of

Above
This Mountain hare and Red grouse sitting on top of a grouse butt share the same natural environment in Scotland.
Mountain hares are extremely vulnerable when the snow has melted and their coats have not yet changed colour. Then their white coats are very obvious against the darkness of the heather

snow in late summer when the hares are in their darker coats can prove equally dangerous for them. Scientists are now of the opinion that the shortening hours of daylight trigger the coat to change to white in winter, rather than falling temperatures as was once thought, although the latter could also be a factor. These transitional times are the best for spotting Mountain hares, for at other times they are excellently camouflaged.

It is these colour changes that earned the Mountain hare the names 'Variable' or 'Varying' hare.

Mountain hare population and habitat

The rise and fall of the Mountain hare population, like that of other species of hares, tends to follow a ten year cycle but it was noted in 1930 that there was a population explosion of them which had been building up since 1910.

They usually live above ground feeding on and sheltering in the heather and natural grasses but have been known to dig shallow holes or utilise the entrances to old rabbit burrows. Lying amidst very thick vegetation or in depressions in the peaty surface, it can appear that they have dug themselves a burrow. There are many places for the Mountain hare to hide among the fissures, rocks and boulders on mountains. Over-

Freak Black Mountain hares

Black Mountain hares have been reported from time to time and in the late 1920s a taxidermist in Inverness was working on three, received from different parts of northern Scotland. It was said that there were black ones living in Caithness at this time

Left
A Mountain hare in summer: their numbers inexplicably built up between 1910 and 1930

grazing and tree planting can affect local populations although young forestry plantations can prove attractive to Mountain hares until the canopy closes over and causes the ground vegetation to die off.

Mountain hare breeding

Breeding normally takes place between March and August and pregnancy lasts about 50 days. One to four litters consisting of one to three young may be produced annually. Survival rate of the young Mountain hare is poor as they have harsh weather to endure, fox predation, and they also have large birds of prey such as the golden eagle and the goshawk to contend with.

Mountain hares are tolerated to a certain degree by moorland keepers because they are an alternative food source to their precious grouse for foxes and birds of prey. Even so,

Left
In some parts of the Scottish Highlands the Mountain hare has to contend with the predations of the golden eagle, in addition to the goshawk, the fox and the wild cat

localised populations may reach pest proportions, especially on well managed grouse moors where predators are controlled and strips of heather which are burned in rotation make food more readily available. Shepherds used to say that three hares ate the equivalent amount of grass and heather to one sheep.

There is always a debate when the subject of interbreeding between the lowland Brown hare and the upland mountain hare is brought up. Certainly their ranges overlap in many areas and many of the Victorian naturalists believed that hybrids existed but this is not an opinion that is generally held today.

A Mountain hare's coat provides excellent camouflage in summer amongst the rocks and heather

Mountain hare culls

In some situations, Mountain hares have to be culled by shooting. When driven with beaters they tend to run uphill, so the shooters have to be placed accordingly.

This is a sport that Europeans, and in particular Italians, are willing to pay for and can provide a modest income for some Scottish sporting estates. The foreign guests are keen to take what they have shot home with them for the table. The Mountain hare, like the Brown hare, has the habit of running a little way when disturbed, then stopping to look round: so it also makes an easy shot with a rifle.

The Irish Hare
Lepus timidus hibernicus

Irish hares are believed to be a sub-species of the Mountain hare. They became isolated in Ireland after the last Ice Age 10,000 years ago. The Irish hare is nearly as big as a Brown hare but its coat is shorter and a much richer colour, particularly in summer. Although Irish hares don't usually turn pure white in winter, it is not uncommon for their fur to become lighter in colour, or part of their coat to change hue. Attempts have been made to introduce Irish hares to the Scottish islands and to England for sport, but they are not a species to be found there now.

Irish hares at airports

About fifty years ago when Irish hare numbers were high, it was not unusual to see gatherings of three or four hundred of them;

Above
The Irish hare: more placid and more adaptable than the Mountain hare from which it is descended

these were called 'herds'. In the 1960s, hundreds of Irish hares lived at the busy Aldergrove airport near Belfast where they gathered in flocks. They seemed to be attracted to the noise, vibrations and smell of the aeroplanes and appeared to be racing them down the runway when they landed or took off. This behaviour by Irish hares was first noted at Nutts Corner airport, which was four miles away from the new Aldergrove airport, but after Aldergrove was opened they are said to have disappeared from Nutts Corner. It is thought they moved to the new airport, such was their liking for planes, and there is still a healthy population there today.

Habitat

Irish hares are seldom seen during the daytime unless flushed but appear to be generally more placid by nature than the Brown hare. They are also more adaptable in their choice of habitat, living where there is mixed farming as well as on moorland and mountain. They can also be found inhabiting the peat bogs scattered across Ireland. These are not wet environments but

Below
The Irish hare is thought to be a sub-species of the British Mountain hare (pictured below) becoming isolated in Ireland after the last Ice Age 10,000 years ago

comparatively dry places covered in white grass and heather and where the cutting of peat has left a very uneven surface.

The hares prefer to lie in rough cover such as rushes, bushes or hedgerows during the day and not to venture out until darkness begins to fall. At night they often travel long distances to seek better feeding areas. It is estimated that Irish hares spend 40% of their time resting and 30% feeding. Their preferred foodstuff is a variety of grasses which is particularly important to the does during lactation. They do not live in burrows but they will hide amongst rocks and boulders or crouch in holes in the ground, just like Mountain hares. The first young of the year are usually born in February.

Irish hare research

Although widespread, the population of hares in Ireland has suffered a decline in the last 30 or so years. In some localities, however, they are still plentiful. Changes in agricultural practices and disturbance, similar changes that have affected the numbers of Brown hares, are mostly blamed. Due to concern over the decline in population, independent research into the

Below
Of the six counties in Northern Ireland, the highest Irish hare population was found in County Antrim and the lowest in County Tyrone

status of the Irish hare has been carried out by the School of Biology and Biochemistry from Queen's University Belfast on behalf of the Northern Ireland Environment and Heritage Service (DoE NI).

Their findings indicate that, despite the low average density of one hare per square km, the overall population has been stable since the mid 1990s. Accurate counting is extremely difficult and their estimate for the total number of Irish hares in Northern Ireland is between 7,000 and 25,000, a considerable discrepancy. The highest density was found on land classed as 'high uplands' where the farming is less intensive and there is reduced disturbance.

Park coursing

Park or enclosed coursing is a popular sport in the whole of Ireland. Unlike the open system for coursing in England and Wales, hares in Ireland are caught in the wild two or three weeks before they are coursed by muzzled greyhounds within an enclosed area from which the hares can escape (see page 142).

Radio-tracked hares

There are two coursing clubs in Northern Ireland. In 2002 a licence to net hares was issued to one of these, the Dungannon Coursing Club and one of the conditions of the licence was that they worked with Queen's University as part of the study into Irish hares. As a result, nine hares netted in Northern Ireland during that winter were fitted with radio collars when they were returned to the wild having been coursed. Batteries on the transmitters lasted for three months and the hare's position could be pin-pointed to within 50 metres.

All the hares were in good condition when they were released in four different areas and they were monitored for five days a week during daylight hours for eleven weeks, although they were rarely seen. One hare lost its collar and two died within the first fortnight. The collar of one of these was found along with some blood and fur and it was presumed that it had been killed by a predator. The cause of death of the second was not known. The other six hares were still alive when monitoring

Irish hares are remarkably adaptable and live in a wide range of habitats, from peat bogs and mountain moorland, to fertile pasture-land and rocky limestone terrain

ceased and were behaving normally. All but one of them had remained within 300 metres of the release site.

A previous radio tracking study in 1996, over a period of twelve months, involved twelve Irish hares that had not been previously coursed; obviously though they had to be caught up to have the collars fitted. Four of these were lost either to mortality or transmitter failure. Similar results have been seen in other experiments.

It would be wrong therefore to assume that the death of the hare in the most recent study was necessarily a result of being coursed. There are many other causes of mortality in hares.

The experiment concluded that there was no evidence that coursing at the current level in Northern Ireland affects either the population or distribution of the Irish hare.

DNA testing

In order to learn more about them, further research is being carried out by the Queen's University Belfast using DNA testing from samples of hair obtained from live hares at coursing meetings, as well as the hair and tissue from road kills.

Professor Ian Montgomery from Queen's University conducting the study believes that hare hunting in its various forms makes a positive contribution to the conservation of hares, through participation in important research, predator control and sympathetic habitat management.

In other words, the benefits outweigh the losses. Records show that together the two coursing clubs and 30 packs of hounds that hunt hares in Northern Ireland only harvest about 30 Irish hares annually, which is less than the Game Conservancy Trust (based in England) estimate that one family of foxes will take in a year. In 2002, the 80,000 shooters in Northern Ireland placed a voluntary ban on shooting Irish hares. It is not in the interest of any sportsman to cause the demise of the quarry he chooses to pursue.

Controversially, and without proper consultation, a temporary Special Protection Order for Irish hares, banning the killing or taking of Irish hares in Northern Ireland, was put into force in January 2004.

Above
Irish hares are seldom seen during the daytime unless flushed and appear to be more placid by nature than the Brown hare

Feeding Habits of the Hare

The Brown hare is an animal of both grassland and arable farmland. In spring and summer, the availability of different herbaceous plants plays an important part in its diet, ensuring that the does are healthy and fertile. Litter size is larger when the doe has a high-quality diet.

The Brown hare has catholic tastes, feeding on a variety of crops. It is wholly vegetarian and is a fastidious feeder, much preferring the lush tender young shoots of corn and clover, different grasses, crops of swedes, turnips, cabbages, lettuces and carrots to rank herbage. The hare is not averse to dining on the bark and shoots of all kinds of trees and shrubs. It also enjoys the delights offered to it by smallholders and market gardeners who grow an even wider range of vegetables! In the flower garden hares can wreak havoc, having a penchant for

The Mountain hare (*above*) can find all its dietary needs amongst the grasses, mosses and heathers on the uplands of Britain. However sometimes it will come down to the lower ground in search of a better source of food

dahlias, carnations, pinks, nasturtiums, wallflowers, primulas, heathers and herbs such as parsley and thyme. In days gone by it was a trick of the old poachers to scatter a few seeds of parsley in a newly-sown crop to attract hares to that particular area later on. Then they would know where to look for them.

In the early 19th century hares were sometimes kept in warrens from where they could be caught up for hunting or coursing, and these warrens were often also sown with parsley. Farmers would sometimes grow a row or two of swedes, which hares love as attractors, alongside another crop, to keep the hares off it and restrict damage.

While almost every countryman welcomes the sight of a hare or two, in excessive numbers they make themselves very unpopular, such is the diversity of their diet. Farm cereal crops and particularly sugar beet can be seriously affected. Rabbit damage is confined to the edge of fields so it is easily seen but a hare will pick here and there and the amount of damage is not

Right
Brown hare feeding on barley. Rabbit damage to crops tends to be at the edges of the field, an area which the hare would associate with danger

Below
Brown hares are normally solitary animals but will sometimes gather together in an area to feed

Left
A Brown hare finds some
greenery in a stubble field after
the harvest

always so obvious. Newly-planted trees and hedges can be
devastated unless they are well protected with wire netting or
plastic tree guards. The forester has little affection for hares
when they turn their attentions to his trees; nor has the gardener
who is forced to fence in his vegetables and flowers.

Although solitary by nature, an abundance of good food
will attract a number of hares to one locality. When fields were
smaller and a diversity of crops were grown, hares did not have
to travel very far from their day-time resting places to feed.

Problems for feeding hares

Today, with vast areas producing a single crop and with the use of modern agricultural techniques, there is less variety of plants for hares to feed on. On some large arable farms all the crops are harvested within a matter of a few weeks. The fields suddenly become bare, resulting in vast areas being devoid of suitable food. Hares may be seen searching the stubble for spilled grain or emerging growth from weeds or germinating corn that has been left behind by the combine.

Sometimes, however, stubble is sprayed with paraquat to kill off this growth, eliminating entirely a potential source of food for the hare and putting it at risk of being poisoned. It is probably a couple of months at least before the land has been cultivated and re-sown and any palatable herbage becomes available. The weeds that once grew freely in farm crops are also now quickly dealt with by spraying the fields with herbicides, thus denying hares the succession of young green growth that they previously relished and need to survive.

Many of the hedges and rough ground which offered shelter have been done away with. Most modern farms are too neat and

Two hares in a cornfield. The modern practice of harvesting a crop from the centre to the outside edge of the field results in fewer deaths of leverets and adult hares than the old method of working from the edge to the centre

Left
Brown hares thrive best where
they have a selection of plants
to choose from. Here a Brown
hare nibbles the heads of barley

tidy to provide a suitable habitat for hares to flourish. However one bonus has been that the planting of more winter corn in autumn has meant that hares have had a nourishing supply of young shoots to feed on through the winter. While the disappearance of autumn stubble has been detrimental to the wild bird population, in some ways it has benefited hares.

Set-aside in arable areas is also proving beneficial by making a wide range of plants and grasses available throughout the year. The uncultivated chalk downlands of southern Britain such as Salisbury Plain also offer the hare a wide variety of plants including native grasses and herbs on which to feed.

However, in other areas on mixed farms, in order to find fresh green food in mid-summer, hares often have to resort to pasture land. Cattle are not tidy grazers and these pastures are preferred as they also offer some cover to hide in during the day.

Opposite page
Natural grassland, a
commodity in increasingly short
supply, provides an excellent
varied diet for the hare, a mix
of weeds and herbs as well as
different species of grasses

71

But pastures occupied by sheep are nibbled very close to the ground and are far less attractive. Most feeding activity for a hare takes place after dark.

An old adage has it that when it comes to the amount of grass or corn a hare will eat, then ten hares equal one sheep or two sacks of corn.

Food for the Mountain hare

While the Brown hare needs variety in its diet, the Mountain hare seems to be able to find all it needs to survive among the natural grasses, mosses and heather found on the hills. However they will sometimes come off the high ground to seek out better quality food in the lower fields, especially in severe weather conditions.

Winter feeding

Abnormally hard weather can make it difficult for any hare to find sufficient food. When the vegetation on the ground is covered with snow, then young trees and bushes are all that can sustain them. Hares can reach up to a metre high. If they can't reach the twigs or small branches, then they resort to eating the bark on the trunk, often right the way round, which results in the tree or bush later dying.

Hares are tempted by the new growth of freshly-planted shrubs and trees and will take the tops out of young fir at any time of the year. Mountain hares for instance can be a real menace where conifer plantations have been planted on the higher moors they inhabit, as has happened in so many parts of Scotland. These hares do not move at first from their home but learn to live within these plantings instead of out on the open hillsides. They are only forced to move when the canopy of the trees becomes so dense that it obliterates the growth beneath and there is nothing left for them to feed on.

Irish hare feeding habits

The Irish hare seems to be more adaptable than either the Brown or Mountain hare. It can be found inhabiting mountainside,

Above
Set-aside in arable areas is also proving beneficial by making a wide range of plants and grasses available throughout the year

rough grazing and lowland pastures and be able to exist in purely grassland areas. Given the choice though, it obviously prefers the better quality of food found growing on arable or in-bye land and will travel considerable distances from its hillside form when dusk falls, to feed on arable land or on such places as golf courses.

Refection

The nutritional value of most plants is comparatively low and some vegetation can be difficult to digest. For hares, like rabbits, to achieve the maximum nutrition from what they eat, they pass the food through their digestive system twice.

Ruminants (cattle and sheep) have the same problem but theirs is resolved by chewing the cud, in other words, regurgitating their food and chewing it again before swallowing it for a second time.

Hares have solved the problem in a different way. Their food passes completely through their digestive system and results in soft oval droppings called 'caecotroph' pellets. These are immediately eaten and then pass through the digestive system for a second time. The resultant droppings are much harder, drier and lighter in colour but still denote the fibrous nature of a hare's diet.

The hare according to Moses

It is very interesting that one of the allusions to hares in the Bible concerns refection. In Leviticus 11 the Lord told Moses and Aaron to tell the children of Israel what beasts on the earth they could and could not eat.

If an animal was cloven hoofed and chewed the cud it was permissible to eat it.

Of the beasts that must not be eaten were those that were cloven footed but didn't chew the cud such as pigs or that chewed the cud but did not have cloven feet such as the camel.

Also prohibited for the latter reason was the coney (rabbit) and the hare:

'And the hare because he cheweth the cud but divideth not the hoof, he is unclean to you.'
'Of their flesh you shall not eat and their carcass shall ye not touch, they are unclean to you.'

There is a further reminder in Deuteronomy 14:

'The camel and the hare and the coney, for they chew the cud but divide not the hoof; therefore they are unclean to you.'

Of course, the hare does not in fact chew the cud. But when it grinds its teeth, a hare could appear to be chewing the cud. It grinds its teeth in order to keep them trimmed and sharp. A hare's teeth, like those of rodents, are continuously growing.

Perhaps Moses or Aaron did know all about refection after all.

Like the rest of its species, the Brown hare is a tooth-grinder and it does this in order to keep its fast-growing teeth level. It is not, as sometimes appears, chewing the cud, like a sheep

Courtship and Reproduction

In Britain, Brown hare courtship begins in January and continues until August or even later. Breeding occurs almost continuously in mild winters and a few leverets may be born as early as January or February. Mountain hares don't start reproducing until March and finish in August or early September.

Bucks are very promiscuous and many may be attracted to a female prior to her being properly in season. A male will stay close to a doe, guarding her, until after mating has taken place. Several males will be drawn to the vicinity of the doe from different directions and there are many scuffles as the males are intent on trying their luck and keep harassing her. Fighting, boxing, scratching and biting takes place and the fur often flies

This seemingly affectionate pose can turn at any moment to boxing as male and female hares come together in the Spring

75

but usually it is the doe who is the aggressor as she tries to fend off their unwanted attentions. Although they normally live a solitary existence, the bucks themselves have a loose social hierarchy and they are aware of where they stand in the pecking order, so that fighting among themselves is kept to a minimum.

A doe is only on heat for a few hours. There is an old saying that the pregnancy of a mare and a hare added together last a year, but a shortage of facts regarding the breeding of hares means there is a difference of opinion as to how long the pregnancy lasts. Hares cannot be successfully domesticated and it is very difficult to observe at close quarters a nocturnal animal in the wild. As a result the precise gestation period of hares is not known. It could be as little as 30 days but the general opinion is that it is about 42 for Brown hares. It is thought that gestation lasts an extra week for Mountain and Irish hares.

Does are usually mated again soon after giving birth and unless she is in peak condition, it is not uncommon for the foetuses to be reabsorbed. Researchers have discovered that it is possible for a Brown hare doe to conceive again while already pregnant. This is known as superfoetation and both the pregnancies apparently continue without either interfering with the other.

Right
Brown hares are weaned when they are about 4-6 weeks old. Brown hares in Britain have three or four litters a year, but few progeny survive

Below
A doe is only on heat for a few hours so there is no time to lose

Above
Although usually solitary animals, a Brown doe on heat may attract several suitors and lead them a merry dance around the fields

Left
A young jack Brown hare tentatively approaches a female

Below left
The acrobatic courtship of group of Brown hares, a time of energetic displays and erratic behaviour

Litters may vary in size from one to seven. Usually between two and four young are born, depending on the time of year. There may be three or four litters annually.

At the height of the breeding season in Spring, researchers have estimated that 100% of does over a year old are pregnant. They do not usually breed in the year in which they were born.

It was recorded in 1840 that an experiment by the Reverend B. Daniel had been conducted into the fecundity of Brown hares. A brace of hares, the doe pregnant at the time, had been released into the protection of a large walled garden, provided with 'proper plants for their sustenance' and left unhindered to their own devices. After a twelve month period the garden was searched and it was found that the original pair had produced a total of 57 offspring! The frequency of litters and the number in them can be greatly affected by the weather. December is probably the least likely month in which to find new born Brown hare leverets.

Hare breeding

The lengthening hours of daylight soon after the winter equinox trigger off reproduction in the Scottish Mountain hare. The does are mated in January. The first of the two or three litters born each year arrive towards the end of February or early in March but rarely survive because the weather is still bad this early in the year and the quality of food available is very poor. Interbreeding between the Mountain hare and the Brown hare where

The dominant male Brown hare will stay close by and guard a doe when she is on heat

their ranges overlap is believed to be possible but rare.

Male hares play no part in raising their offspring.

Leverets are born on top of the ground and no nest is made. Despite their inherent wariness, it is not unusual to find that Brown hares give birth to their young in close proximity to humans, even in the flower borders or vegetable beds of country cottage gardens.

The leverets are born fully furred, have their eyes open and within a short time become active and able to run. At first the colour of a leveret's eyes is dark blue, almost black, but they soon change to a rich golden colour.

After a few hours the doe spreads her litter out in different places to lessen the likelihood of predators finding and killing all of them. This she probably does by carrying them in her mouth. The odd clump of rough grass in pasture fields may be the only available cover. It is rare for leverets to be hidden in hedges as this is the haunt of stoats and foxes, two of the leverets' worst enemies.

At this early stage in their lives, leverets are extremely vulnerable, relying on keeping still and camouflage for their sole protection.

The doe only visits once a day after dark to suckle them for

A doe fends off the unwanted attention of a male in springtime

Pregnant twice

One of the many astounding things about a hare is that it is possible for a Brown hare doe to conceive again while already pregnant. This is known as superfoetation and both the pregnancies apparently continue without either interfering with the other.

a short period which she does in a sitting position. Opinion is divided over whether the leverets gather together to suckle at what might be the place where they were born, whether the doe calls them up, or whether she visits each one individually. The general consensus is that she calls them to her, as there have been many sightings of more than one suckling at a time.

It has been observed that, when approaching or leaving her young, she goes through the same antics to cover up her scent as when she goes to her form: back-tracking, leaping etc. The rest of the time she keeps her distance from the leverets but stays in the vicinity and will fight for their safety should they be

Less than one hour old. A fully furred leveret surveys his new world. He will soon need to find cover in the long grass, safe from the predatory attentions of hawks, stoats and foxes.

at risk, even attacking cows or sheep if they approach too close.

Leverets begin to eat grass after 10 to 14 days and are fully weaned at about 4–6 weeks old, from which time they have to fend for themselves. Weaning is often brought about by the imminent birth of another litter. Leverets sometimes gather together in groups when they are a few weeks old.

Young hares are mature at about six months of age but do not normally breed in the year in which they were born.

Cowper and his three pet hares

Books written a hundred years ago suggest that leverets were quite easy to rear artificially but modern opinion differ with those findings. The poet William Cowper kept three Brown hares as pets: Puss, Tiney and Bess. Despite their names they were in fact all males.

Bess was always tame but died soon after he was fully grown. Tiney never did become tame and would strike out with his forefeet, grunt and bite if anyone tried to handle him. He lived until he was eight years and five months old and Cowper described him as being 'the surliest of his kind.' Puss, however, grew to be tame and was delightful to have as a pet. Apparently he was happy to be carried around and could be let out into the garden. In fact he would ask to be taken out there by drumming on Cowper's knee or pulling at the skirts of his coat with his teeth. Puss lived until he was eleven years and eleven months

Left
A jack Brown hare, close on the heels of a female in season

This orphaned leveret was successfully hand-reared by Jill Mason and released into the wild after 8 weeks. Fortunately, during the bottle-feeding period the hare never became tame and this enabled him to adapt quickly to living in the wild

old and an account of his hares, written by Cowper himself, appeared in the *Gentleman's Magazine* on the 28 May 1784 and filled seven pages. He observed that they would investigate everything, using particularly their sense of smell. He recounts that they detested some people but were immediately attracted to a miller who visited. Presumably they were drawn to him by the pleasant smell of wheat and flour on his clothes.

Other hand-reared hares

Another person who kept a doe for more than two years recorded that he found her to be most active after dark and very sensitive to changes in atmospheric pressure (changeable weather).

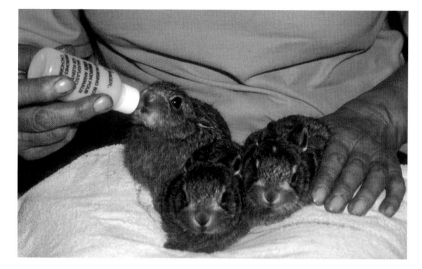

Left
Leverets found in fields or moors are seldom 'abandoned' and should not be touched or moved. The mother hare will not be far away and will return to feed them once a day after dark. Just occasionally, situations occur in which it is known for certain that they are orphans. Such was the case with these three leverets which were bottle-reared by the author. Sadly only one made it to weaning and release. They are notoriously difficult animals to rear in captivity

W.B. Yeats in his poem *Two Songs of a Fool* wrote 'A speckled cat and a tame hare eat at my hearthstone and sleep there.' There are other accounts of young hares being fostered on to cats feeding kittens, and of older hares living quite happily alongside pet dogs and even being taught to do tricks. J.J. Manley, author of *Notes on Game and Game Shooting* (1881), commented that 'many of us have seen performing hares in the London streets,' although he himself had not been able to tame one.

It is generally agreed today that young hares are difficult to rear, even when they are artificially fed on a milk substitute such as cat's milk replacement. If they do survive, they usually prove to be very highly strung. A single hare is much more likely to be tamed than when two or three are reared together.

Commercial breeding of Brown hares in captivity

The Brown hare has never been domesticated and because they are so highly strung, their behaviour in captivity is significantly different to that in the wild. Captive breeding is technically possible but because of the very nature of the animal it would be extremely difficult for it to be viable as an economic, large scale commercial venture. Only two or three litters of up to four are normally produced each year and heavy losses are likely through stress, disease, reproductive problems and high death rates in leverets prior to weaning.

There is a report (1963) of five farms in the Ukraine having been established to breed hares for export to western Europe although it doesn't say under what conditions they were kept. Brown hare breeding ventures have also been established in northern Italy and France as well as in some other Eastern European countries. These however were small enterprises and the hares were not grown to the weights required for meat production but kept for either research projects or for reintroduction to the wild.

Many young ones are sold to stock hunting or game parks several weeks before the hunting season begins, allowing them the time to become acclimatised, familiar with their environment in the wild and to develop natural behavioural patterns.

In both Italy and England, in the 1800s, Brown hares were bred in warrens for sporting purposes. These warrens were enclosed areas covering several acres so the hares were free range and able to live in semi-natural conditions.

Europe is the major market for hare meat and the big demand is met by imports from Argentina and Chile to supplement local supplies. This South American meat comes from shot wild hares that have been processed, vacuum packed and frozen.

There is also a small world market for hare pelts to supply hat and clothes-wear manufacturers, particularly those making trimmings and Akubra-style hats.

A rare moment captured in this photograph of a procession of 'Mad' March hares

Enemies of the Hare

Of all the predators in Britain, by far the most damaging to hares is the fox. This is why hares are most likely to thrive on estates where gamekeepers are employed, because they kill foxes in order to protect their game birds.

The Mammal Research Unit recently carried out a five-year study funded by DEFRA which showed that hares are rarely observed where foxes were seen frequently. It is estimated that a family of foxes can account for 33 adult hares in the course of a year. The badger population is exploding at present, and they are now prevalent in areas where once they were rare. Badgers kill a lot of leverets and may be affecting the hare population more than is realised.

Leverets are also very susceptible to predation by stoats, another species which are controlled by a declining band of gamekeepers.

Mink are a comparatively new threat and are becoming widespread across Britain and Ireland. These will hunt some

DEFRA reports that hares are scarce where foxes (left) are prevalent. It is estimated that a family of foxes can kill as many as 33 adult hares each year

distance away from the rivers and streams where they live, also posing yet another serious threat to young hares. Even though they are small stoats and mink will tackle hares that are full grown.

Their even smaller cousin the weasel will prey on young leverets as will cats both feral and domestic.

Hares are hunted by dogs using either scent or sight. Sight or gaze hounds such as salukis, greyhounds, deerhounds and whippets rely purely on speed to catch their quarry. Bassetts, beagles and harriers do not have the speed of gaze hounds but a good nose to hunt by scent, and stamina, enabling them to follow a hare for a long distance.

On the other hand lurchers combine the qualities of scenting ability, stamina, intelligence and speed. A lurcher may be a mix of many different breeds or merely a crossbred so these qualities may show themselves in differing ratios according to the breeding and they can become very clever at catching hares. It is not only the specialists-bred dogs, though, which pose a threat to hares. Almost any breed from the farm collie to a pet Jack Russell can quite easily come upon a young hare crouched

Left
Agricultural chemicals sprayed on the land and crops may in some instances be harmful to hares

Bottom left
Leverets are at great risk if they are hidden in grass fields cut for silage

motionless in its hiding place and kill it. Few dogs of any breeding can resist the temptation to chase fur, whether it be a rabbit or hare. This temptation is especially great for gun dogs who are worked on game birds in an environment where ground game also abounds. They may well be sent to collect a dead or wounded hare but are expected to ignore an unshot one. It is a well trained dog that will stand still and watch one departing.

Across the world, hare is on the menu of most predators. In Europe, besides foxes, there are wolves and lynx. North America also has coyotes. Polar bears in the Arctic regions will snack on a hare and in Africa, snakes, big cats and hyenas will do the same. Leverets of course have even more enemies.

The larger wild birds of prey everywhere also take their toll of hares. In Britain Brown hares are at risk from the likes of hen

Not for sale

Hares can be killed at any time of the year but not offered for sale during certain months. Genuine sportsmen operate a voluntary close season from April until September (the main breeding season) but illegal poachers pay no heed to moral obligations.

Left
In the 21st century, the hare probably faces its biggest threat from man. Railways, motor cars and high speed farm machinery account for thousands of hare deaths each year. This juvenile hare was run over on a normally quiet Norfolk lane

harriers, buzzards and goshawks, while Mountain hares also have golden eagles to contend with. In other countries there are many species of birds of prey including large owls such as the Great Grey and the Snowy owl in northern regions and the eagles and buzzards of Africa and India.

Within hours of the birth a doe hare disperses her litter. The leveret's only defence at this time is to remain hidden in thick cover

Modern threats to the hare

The British hare probably faces its biggest threat, though, from man. Railways, motor cars and high speed farm machinery account for thousands of hare deaths each year. Even before farming became so mechanised, a few would be killed by the scythes of farmworkers cutting corn or grass for hay. Crouching down and relying on camouflage when faced with danger offers little protection from a sharp blade.

Agricultural chemicals too can also be very harmful, particularly when stubble fields in which hares have been feeding on the new growth are treated with paraquat-based sprays.

While predator control by gamekeepers can greatly benefit the hare population, it can also prove detrimental if snares are set for foxes or rabbits. Unless great care is taken in the choice of places where snares are set, it is likely that hares may also be caught, for they often use the same runs as a fox through a hedge or under a fence. Lamping at night with a spotlight and a rifle has become the most popular way of dealing with foxes in many areas. This is selective, as the quarry can be easily identified, so hares are no doubt benefiting from this method of fox control, providing they are not also the quarry.

Poaching

Poaching has always been a problem with hares. In the olden days it was a serious offence but a hare was worth a lot of money to a poor man trying to feed his family and many took the risk. In 1895, a poacher could get 2/6d for a good hare which would then have constituted a large percentage of his weekly wage.

Now modern poaching is still about money, but today the income is not from the sale of the carcass but from the bets made on running dogs, mainly lurchers or greyhounds. Some unscrupulous people not only indiscriminately take a significant number of hares at any time of the year but they also think nothing of driving across crops, damaging hedges and fences and threatening the well-being of anyone who approaches them.

This illegal poaching results in some landowners and farmers keeping hare numbers to an absolute minimum to avoid attracting these undesirables to the farm in the first place. This is a double-edged sword as far as the hare is concerned. Not only are numbers reduced because of the direct action of illegal coursing but also by the destruction of the hare population by farmers who see no other answer to the problem.

Another sport, which is tantamount to poaching if permission has not been given, is hare lamping at night. This is when a strong beam of a light is directed at the hare and it is then shot, or a dog is released to catch the transfixed animal, or it may be driven towards a fixed net. Rural crimes such as poaching are often regarded as low-priority for over-stretched rural police forces and are rarely dealt with efficiently by the courts.

Optimum numbers

Disease is more prevalent where populations are high. The winter cull to prevent crop damage on farms where numbers are great indirectly helps to control the spread of disease. Inevitably though, hares may ail if the weather is very wet, or if they are forced to eat an unsuitable diet, either from lack of food or as a result of the use of agricultural chemicals

Young Brown hares have to fend for themselves once they are weaned at the age of 4–6 weeks

Disease and Hares

Wild Brown hares in Britain suffer from a number of diseases and the situation is aggravated in the wetter regions of the country. Most diseases have little effect on the hare and only cause illness or death if the animal is exposed to stress resulting from bad weather, a poor diet or over-population.

Disease in hares is not a new thing. There are reports of a great many hares dying in Eisvold (Norway) in the autumn of 1882 due to 'congestion of the air passages'. Severe losses were also recorded in Alsace soon afterwards, when deaths were said to have been caused by a parasitic disease.

More recently, research in France and Scandinavia has identified *Tularaemia*, a disease of rodents; and *Brucellosis*, a disease of cattle, goats and pigs, in hares. Much more routine diagnostic work and research into hares has been carried out on the Continent than in Britain. Most of the work in the UK has been undertaken by a group from Bristol University and another at Oxford who have been studying the ecological aspects of hares for many years.

Neither pets nor pests

Hares are not regarded as pets or pests in Britain. As hares have never been involved in any major health scares in Britain, there has been little motivation or necessity for anyone to instigate expensive research and study

93

Game Conservancy Trust research

Studies on hares in Britain are usually a spin-off from research being carried out on another species, such as the work the Game Conservancy Trust are currently undertaking on red grouse in Scotland. They have been carrying out extensive research into the welfare of grouse and the interaction between them and sheep, red deer and Mountain hares. Hares, in common with the sheep and red deer, are frequently host to ticks which play a part in the transmission of Louping Ill, a disease that can seriously debilitate grouse and cause up to 80% mortality in grouse chicks.

Another common problem these animals share is one of intestinal worms. Part of the Game Conservancy Trust's work has involved catching up a number of Mountain hares, dosing the females with an anthelmintic (wormer) and then monitoring them afterwards to ascertain what effect gut parasites have on hare survival and pregnancy rates. Their research so far has concluded that the parasitic worm *Trichostrongylus retortaeformis* found in the gut of mountain hares has little detrimental effect on the hare's survival but substantially reduces fecundity. This could be the cause of fluctuations (up to tenfold) in the population that naturally occurs on a seven-to-ten year cycle.

The findings of Katherine Whitwell

Katherine Whitwell FRCVS is a horse pathologist in Newmarket who became involved indirectly with hare diseases through

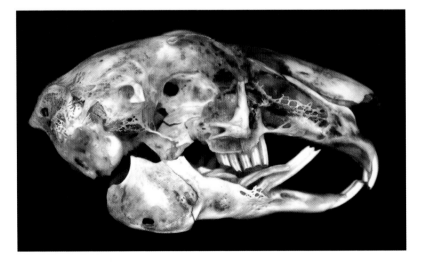

Left
One study into the diseases of hares found that overgrown cheek teeth resulted in death due to starvation in 2% of a random sample of one hundred Brown hares found dead in East Anglia

investigating cases of grass sickness (*Equine dysautonomia*) in horses in the early 1990s. As part of her work, she carried out post-mortems on five hundred wild hares picked up dead, mostly by gamekeepers. Her research involved only Brown hares from East Anglia and the following results were from the first hundred she examined.

She found that the most common cause of death was *Coccidiosis* which accounted for 28% of the deaths. This is a parasitic disease of the gut that is present in most hares, but in young leverets which have not had time to build up any immunity, and those under stress, the infection may rapidly multiply to such an extent that it results in death. It is aggravated by wet weather and autumn is the time of year that *Coccidiosis* is most likely to be a problem. A hare with this disease will become emaciated before it dies.

The second most prolific cause of death was Grass Sickness-like disease (*Leporine dysautonomia*) at 24% but Katherine was unable to establish a direct link to equine grass sickness. This disease is thought to be caused by a bacterial toxin that attacks the nervous system, making it impossible for the hare to eat or swallow, causing the stomach and bowels to become clogged up so they do not function. The hare consequently becomes dehydrated and wastes away. Obvious symptoms are wetness around the mouth, with a very hard abdomen, due to impaction of the large bowel.

18% of deaths were caused by bacterial infections such as *Yersinia pseudotuberculosis*, *Pasteurella*, *Staphylococcus* and *E coli* (*Escherichia Coli*). *Amyloidosis*, a secondary effect of illness caused by bacterial infection, accounted for a further 10%.

Abdominal conditions such as *Typhlitis,* duodenal ulcer, and *Stenosis* of the small intestine caused 7% losses.

Another 6% of deaths were caused by EBHS (European Brown Hare Syndrome) a viral disease which causes hepatitis and leads to rapid death. This disease is akin to RHD (Rabbit Haemorrhagic Disease) which has almost wiped out rabbits in some areas. Outbreaks of EBHS affect hares every few years and devastate populations. The survivors develop an immunity to the disease but after a few years, fresh generations have no resistance to it and are extremely vulnerable when a new outbreak occurs.

Strengthening the gene pool: a female hare 'boxes' away a male suitor with whom she chooses not to mate. In this way, only the healthiest will procreate

Cancer (*Neoplasia*) accounted for 2% and a further 2% of deaths were caused by starvation as a result of the cheek (back) teeth being deformed and becoming overgrown. The teeth of a hare grow continuously and if the jaw is slightly deformed for any reason, the molars don't get worn down evenly and eventually grow very long. An accurate diagnosis of cause of death was not possible on the remaining 3%.

Of course not all hare diseases are fatal, although they may weaken the hare sufficiently to make them succumb to other infections which can result in death. Cases of hare syphilis (*Treponema*) are not fatal but result in lesions around the mouth.

Intestinal worms (*Endoparasites*) are quite common and tapeworms present in large numbers can cause illness. Lung worm and liver fluke affect hares in some countries but have not been reported in Britain. Mites, sucking lice, rabbit, hedgehog and rat fleas (*Ectoparasites*) have all been found on hares and both Mountain and Brown hares suffer from infestations of ticks which can be quite heavy in some areas.

Poisoning from eating plants is rare although in the past it was thought that hares could be poisoned by broom which in some places was the only green plant hares could find showing when there was abnormally deep snow.

It appears that where there is a high density of hares, the population will peak at a certain level, after which the death-rate increases. This means that the reproduction rate of hares on estates where numbers are regularly controlled by culling may exceed that on estates where they are left untouched.

Above
A Brown hare will sit out the worst of the weather in its form in an open field. Abnormally deep snow conditions, such as this, may force hares to eat plants that could be toxic to them

The good news

Hares, unlike rabbits, are resistant to myxomatosis and rarely show any clinical signs of the disease

Legends and Myths
of the Hare

In pre-Christian times, the hare was sacred to heathens and played a big part in pagan religious beliefs. Later on the hare became the subject of superstitions and even today there are still unusual theories relating to hares that old countrymen pass on. For example, leverets are very often born with a white spot or small stripe on their foreheads, and this mark usually soon disappears. Some countryfolk would tell you that it is sign that there were more than two born in the litter, maybe three or four.

Others swear that hares sleep with their eyes open or that a doe runs with her ears flat against her back, while a buck has one ear forward and the other back when it flees.

When a hare is lying in its form, some also reckon they can tell the sexes apart, claiming that the buck lies with its ears firmly together tight along its back while a doe has them open and distended. Another old saying is that a hare always lies within sound of a dog's bark.

For centuries the hare has been a source of myth and superstition

97

The adages used of countrymen today are insignificant compared with the fables, myths, superstitions and religious beliefs that filled the lives of our forefathers. Because they have been handed down through generations, slightly differing versions of the same tales abound but even so, many cultures around the world share similar hare stories. No doubt the beliefs originated from coincidences but in time became deeply embedded within the souls of our ancestors.

Many centuries ago man relied on his skill as a hunter to survive, and the mannerisms of his quarry were often acted out in rituals. Even well into the last century and possibly even today, the more so-called 'primitive' native tribes inhabiting some of the most remote places of the world still did this. If the hare was their quarry then their ceremonies would involve wearing a headdress with long ears. Certainly it once happened in Europe.

Native Americans and the hare

The native American tribes of North America also utilised hares or jackrabbits as a source of food. Communal hunts organised by the Shoshoni and Paiutes from the Idaho/Wyoming regions involved religious ceremonies out of respect to the animal and to appease the spirits so that the source of their food would be sustained. These tribes recognised their dependence on the hare as well as antelope for both food and clothing. Forty hare skins were needed to make a native American garment so only those of high status would be able to wear one. The rest could only be spared a skin or two with which to protect their legs and feet.

In 1800 there were 53 tribes of native Americans in California, a state that embraces deserts and alpine habitats as well as diverse regions in between. Here there were Snowshoe hares and white-tailed jackrabbits to be hunted.

In areas of the far north and across Canada, tribes such as the 'Hare', the 'Cree', and the 'Chipewyan' also caught rabbits and hares in snares fashioned from strips of raw hide or dead fall traps. Meat accounted for a high proportion of their diet although that of a rabbit or hare does not carry sufficient fat needed to supply the calorie intake that these sub-arctic tribes

Tribal respect

Many sub-arctic tribes trapped fur to trade for other items and managed their resources with respect, only reaping the harvest in November and December when the the animals were mature and at their peak, unlike the invading white trappers who trapped the whole year round

required to sustain them, so its meat was of little value to them for much of the time. In fact, they had a saying that you could 'starve to death on rabbits.'

The pelts were used to make clothes and blankets. Many sub-arctic tribes trapped fur to trade for other items and managed their resources with respect, only reaping the harvest in November and December when the the animals were mature and at their peak, unlike the invading white trappers who trapped the whole year round.

During January and February when the weather was at its worst and there was very little daylight, the skins would be processed. This was a time for story-telling and a time when legends could be kept alive. The Montagnais hunters of Newfoundland would sometimes invoke the tales by holding a hare's shoulderblade bone over a fire and then interpreting the resulting pattern of cracks, breaks and blackened spots. This ancient custom is still enacted and was filmed as recently as 1989.

Inevitably an empathy with the hare developed through sharing the same environment and hardships.

Above
Most of the sightings early man had of hares would have been by the moonlight

Origins of the name

The English word 'hare' is said to come from the Anglo-Saxon word 'Hara'. A similar word is also found in some other languages including Dutch, Swedish and old German. After centuries of very little change in people's lives, the last few decades have seen a distancing from the myths and superstitions that once abounded. Far fewer people now have everyday contact with the countryside. The plethora of current information dispensed through TV, films and magazines dispels many of the mysteries that fed the uninformed minds of previous generations. Scientific findings now mean that many of the things our ancestors feared or believed in seem ridiculous to us and yet to them they were all too real.

Worldwide hare fables

The hare appears in fables across the world, even as far away as Japan. In ancient Egypt the moon god Un-Nefer is depicted as a hare-headed figure and the form of a hare was applied in hieroglyphics. In North America the hare was associated with the dawn and the Algonquin Indians believed it was the creator of the sun, moon and earth and ruler of the winds; in fact it was their equivalent of the Christian God. Like the neighbouring Iroquian they believed that man was part of the web of the natural world and that the woodlands and earth could not be exploited or owned.

In the Middle East the female hare Akrasha, through her association with the moon and six stars known as Al Thurayya, was thought to drive away evil djinns. Cultures in many countries around the world as far apart as India, China, Mexico, Africa, North America, Scandinavia and Europe linked the hare symbolically with the moon, the dawn, the seasons, madness and sometimes with fire. In Britain the full moon in April was called the 'hare moon'.

The Chinese calendar, instigated by Emperor Huang Ti in 2637 BC, worked out a lunar cycle over twelve years, each year

The barber and the hare from 'The Three Brothers', a story by the Grimm brothers.
Three sons learn different trades to impress their father. The one who trained as a barber here displays his skills by trimming a passing hare's whiskers expertly, without inflicting a single scratch.
(illustrated by
Ruth Koser-Michaels, 1937)

101

of which is represented symbolically by twelve different creatures one of which is the rabbit or hare. The lunar calendar works on a regular twenty eight day cycle and therefore does not correspond to our western solar calendar. The last Chinese year of the Rabbit/Hare extended from 16 February 1999 until 4 February 2000. The Rabbit/Hare is also represented as a month in the year and corresponds to the solar sign of Pisces covering the period from 20 February–20 March.

Those born under the sign of the Rabbit/Hare are said to have many virtues and to be lucky in business but they may also be moody, over-sensitive to criticism, cunning and even ruthless at times. And because of the hare association, it is also said that it may be difficult to know what they are thinking.

Chinese culture did not often associate the hare with bad omens or ill fortune as was the case in so many other countries.

Below
A Brown hare dozing in the sunshine dispels the myth that a hare sleeps with its eyes open

In Chinese mythology, the hare symbolised longevity and the Chinese moon is regarded as not having a man in it but instead a hare standing near a rock beside a Cassia tree holding the 'elixir of mortality'.

Hares and the moon

During the Chinese mid-autumn festival, children traditionally carried to the tops of hills lighted paper lanterns made in the image of a hare and from this vantage point they could admire and watch the immortal Moon Hare.

In some countries, people see an image of a hare in the moon, rather than 'the Man in the Moon' and a hare appears with a crescent moon in icons of the Hindu and Buddhist faiths.

In one religious myth, a hare is said to have sacrificed itself by jumping into a fire in order to feed the Buddha when he was starving.

The moon itself must have been a potent symbol to ancient man because, unlike the sun, it didn't follow a daily pattern but instead it seemed to die and be reborn again. Like hares, the moon is inconsistent. The hare stood as an emblem of reproduction, birth, growth and death before being reborn. Probably nearly all the sightings early man had of the nocturnal hares would have been by moonlight. The word 'lunacy' is derived from lunar meaning relating to the moon, and 'lunatic' can also be descriptive of hares.

Classical hares

Hares also appear in Roman and Greek mythology, where they are often associated with the Gods. There is also the usual misinformation: there is evidence that the Romans believed that hares ate snow!

Many hare artefacts have been found relating to the Roman occupation of England between the first and fifth centuries AD. For example, a tombstone of a 25-year-old Roman soldier was discovered in Northumberland with the image of a hare engraved above the inscription and a Castor-ware pot showing a hare coursing scene has been found in Cambridgeshire.

Lunar Hare

Before the advent of electricity, man will have seen hares most frequently during a full moon. The hare has thus always been associated with the moon, and via that with monthly fertility and with the 'lunacy' of the mad March hare

Hares in art and jewellery

The Salisbury and South Wiltshire Museum have on display a brooch in the form of a hare that dates back to the first century. It is a flat 'plate brooch' in which the hare's eye and part of its body has been hollowed out and filled with red enamel. It was unearthed near Salisbury.

Several small folding knives decorated with images of a hare and dog have also been found in England. The triangular iron blade is joined to a copper alloy handle by an iron rivet. The handle depicts a running hare being seized from behind by a pursuing hound. One is on display at the Corinium Museum in Cirencester as is a large, fourth century floor mosaic that features a hare in the centre.

Throughout the Dark Ages, animals and birds that were admired and respected for their individual attributes, such as the hare's speed, were often symbolically depicted in carvings, sculptures, paintings and even jewellery.

A Cornish myth

In Cornwall it was believed that if a girl died of grief after having been betrayed by her lover, she would turn into a white hare and her spirit would return to haunt him

Misconceptions

The Saxons who colonised Britain after the Romans worshipped a hare goddess. In later years, because of this pagan connection and the way hares scream and stand on their hind legs to fight, they acquired a reputation for being sinister and connected with evil. In Ireland, the Irish hare was said to turn into a banshee when it was cornered by dogs.

Country people in Wales, in common with many other parts of the world used to think that hares changed sex every month. Related to this tale is a fable. When the animals left Noah's Ark at the end of the great flood, the doe hare fell in the water and drowned, so God gave the buck the ability to give birth, and consequently people believed that the male hare was able to give birth.

Another version of the same story is that Noah cut off the female hare's foot to plug a hole in the Ark and she subsequently died.

In the Middle East it was thought that the sex of 'Akhuzuz' (the male hare) alternated from year to year.

Above
An early French postcard dated 1906. The postcard depicts 'Easter Bunnies' with Easter eggs – a Christian adaptation of the pagan association of the hare with the Spring

Left
This church in the Tanat Valley, North Wales, is dedicated to St Melangell the patron saint of hares. Her Latin name was Monacella

Witches and hares

As long ago as the twelfth century, and even up until the nineteenth, there was a commonly-held belief that hares could turn into witches and back again at will. These so called 'witch-hares' stole milk from cows and sheep in the fields and did other damage and could only be caught by a black greyhound or shot with a silver bullet or an arrow barbed with silver. The son of a witch who dabbled in the black art was called 'The Hare Smith'.

As well as thinking a hare could be a witch, it was also thought of as the devil in disguise.

There is a folk tale of a hunter chasing a hare but only wounding it. He followed until it disappeared inside a house. When he looked inside he found an old woman very much out of breath and bleeding from the leg. There are other similar stories of young girls and old women who were believed to be local witches sustaining identical injuries to those of the hunted hare. This story occurs over and over again in different cultures, in slightly different versions.

The word 'witch' today conjures up a vision of an old hag casting spells and who, if crossed, sticks pins in effigies. But a witch can also be taken to mean someone with a vast knowledge of traditional cures, even if she does live alone in a wood with a cat for company! It was not until 1951 that the Witchcraft Act of 1736 was repealed. Even in this day and age there is a surprisingly large

Below
The sign outside the church of St Melangell at Pennant Melangell has the symbol of a hare carved on it

following of paganism, covering a multitude of beliefs. Many still embrace a closeness with nature and the symbolic meanings of those things connected with it. An article by Jan Millington appeared in the Northern Pagan Archive magazine *Merrymet* in 2003 suggesting that the hare is symbolic of our relationship with the land and could be identified with the need to temper our use of the natural environment. 'We need to listen to what Hare tells us about our Land and our relationship to the Land'. A sentiment shared by many.

Ancient Britons and the hare

Our ancestors depended on the countryside and its wildlife for their survival. This inevitably meant that for the Ancient Britons many animals became entwined with their religious beliefs and some animals were considered sacred. The hare was sacred to the Earth Mother or the White Goddess who was the provider of all things, and this led to the hare being worshipped across the world in various modes and under different names. One hare deity was as the Roman goddess Diana - the huntress. Hunting the hare, an animal that was sacred to the Ancient Britons, was taboo.

The Celts who worshipped the hare would not eat its meat nor kill them except at the Beltane festival. There were three Celtic Springtime festivals of which Beltane was the last, held on 1st May, and traditionally marked the arrival of summer.

Above
A Swiss Easter card depicting a hare hiding the eggs

Left
An early German postcard with the greeting for Happy Easter. The German word 'Ostern' and the English word 'Easter' derived from the name of a heathen goddess called Eostre unlike other European countries which named the Holy Festival after the Hebrew word 'Pasah'

Origins of the Easter bunny

The Anglo-Saxons too had a deep respect for the hare but they hunted it only at the time of their Spring festival which was sacred to their goddess Eostre. Before a hare could be reborn it had to die, which was why it was sacrificed by being hunted and the flesh eaten. Eostre was the goddess of spring, moon and the dawn and the hare was her sacred animal.

The Anglo Saxons believed that the hare laid eggs (a symbol of fertility) to signify the imminence of the year's rebirth. Eostre was often portrayed as a woman with a hare's head. Each year, our ancestors must have feared that the hardships of a cold dark winter would not come to an end, so they greeted the changing of the season with great relief and joy.

This Spring festival was also a celebration of fertility just as everything in nature began to come to life again and was held around 21 March, the time of the vernal equinox. The Spring festival was called Eastre or Aestre which evolved from the name of the goddess Eostre and is sometimes known as Oestre, Ostaris or Ostara. The Christian religious festival of Easter is timed to replace this pagan celebration.

Today's Easter bunny was actually the hare of pagan times.

Leverets are often born with a white spot or stripe on their foreheads. Some countryfolk used to say that this was a sign that there were more than two in the litter

The hare was substituted by the rabbit because Christians did not want to be associated in any way with the hare, a symbol of the old paganism.

The modern custom of children searching for Easter eggs hidden in hares' nests has evolved from this pagan belief. Painted eggs have been exchanged symbolically at the Spring festival since ancient times by the Greeks, Romans, Chinese and Persians. It is interesting to note that the Saxons who invaded Britain after the Romans withdrew, came from Germany and, unlike other Mediterranean European cultures who named this holy festival after the Hebrew word 'pasah', Britain and Germany derived the names 'Easter' and the German 'Ostern' from the heathen goddess Eostre.

The patron saint of hares

In Wales, 27 May is the feast day of Saint Melangell. She is one of the early Abbesses to come to Britain, a Celtic virgin who settled in the Tanat valley in north Wales more than 1,400 years ago, after having come from Ireland. Her Latin name is Monacella.

There is a legend that in AD 604 an illustrious Welsh prince from Powys was hunting in a place called Pennant when his hounds startled a hare and gave chase. He followed them into a thicket of brambles and thorns where he found a beautiful maiden in divine contemplation and perceived that the hare had taken refuge beneath the hem of her garments.

The Prince urged his hounds on but they fled howling. He was moved by her piety and serenity and impressed that Melangell had provided refuge for the little wild hare that his hounds had been pursuing. He endowed her with land in the valley as a place of sanctuary for the service of God and to be a perpetual asylum and refuge.

She spent the rest of her days in that lonely spot where she founded a religious community and wrought miracles for those with pure hearts who sought refuge there. She became the patron saint of hares and even today the local hunters of the Tanat Valley are said not to shoot them. Celtic Christians felt an affinity with the natural world.

Above
Although hares are usually associated with evil, mystery and madness, some people believed that carrying a hare's paw in their right pocket would prevent them suffering from cramp or rheumatism. The diarist Samuel Pepys is said to have carried the right foot of one in his pocket as a cure for colic, writing, *'It is a strange thing how fancy works, for I no sooner handled his jointed foot but I became very well and so continue.'*

This small 1st century Roman brooch, just 3.25 centimetres long, once held red enamel in the recessed area of the body and eye. It was found at Stockton Earthworks and is now on display at the Salisbury and South Wiltshire Museum.

(*Photograph reproduced by kind permission of the Salisbury and South Wiltshire Museum*)

Like that hare of long ago, pilgrims from all nations and denominations seek peace and tranquillity even today with St Melangell at the church dedicated to her and the Centre named after her at Pennant Melangell in north Wales.

Romans brought the Christian religion with them and it was very slow to spread but by 735AD Christianity had travelled the length and breadth of Britain. When the new faith eventually became established, pagans who kept their old beliefs in Medieval Britain were burned at the stake, labelled as witches. It is surprising therefore that Christian Saints in heaven are sometimes portrayed as hares nibbling at grapes, despite the animal's connection with paganism.

Hares and superstitions

There are many superstitions relating to hares, the majority of which are associated with bad luck and misfortune. In 60AD, Queen Boudicea is said to have prayed to a hare goddess before going in to battle with the Romans.

There is even a story that before planning which route her army should take, she released a hare from beneath her gown so that it would show her which way to go. It is not known whether this was prior to her triumphs at Colchester, London and St Albans or maybe it was the battle near Towcester when she and her army were defeated.

Melangell provides refuge for the little wild hare that the hounds were pursuing. The hunter, a Welsh prince was so impressed by this serene maiden that he granted her land on which she founded a religious community. Melangell, whose Latin name is Monacella, is today the patron saint of hares

Bad omens

Another harbinger of ill fortune was the hare that appeared amidst his soldiers when James IV of Scotland was holding a council of war in Northumberland in September 1513 prior to the Battle of Flodden Field. Despite a volley of missiles aimed at it by those present, the hare escaped. James subsequently suffered a terrible defeat and was killed by English troops under the command of the Earl of Surrey on September 9th. It was considered so unlucky if a hare crossed the path of a man setting off on a journey that many a traveller would return home and start afresh. Perhaps James IV should have heeded this particular superstition.

It was bad news too if a hare circled in an anti-clockwise direction. In northern England it was unlucky to see one jumping on to a wall or to dream about one because it was a sign that the dreamer had enemies and misfortune or death would befall someone in his family.

It was a very bad omen if a hare crossed the road in front of a wedding procession. There was also a superstition that a hare could be a fairy that had snatched a dead child from its coffin. A hare running down the main street of a village meant there would be a fire.

It was thought that if a pregnant woman ate a hare then she would miscarry. Hares were also said to be responsible for babies being born disfigured by a harelip, if the pregnant mother had seen one. To avoid this happening, she had to either rip one of her garments or slit the offending creature's ear. The former option was probably the easiest. A fractious baby could be soothed by being given a little jelly made from the brain of a hare.

In Cornwall it was believed that a girl who died of grief after having been betrayed by her lover would turn into a white hare and her spirit would return to haunt him. It was also thought any white hare brought bad luck as they were said to be the returning soul of someone who had died in tragic circumstances.

Sailors when they were at sea would never speak of a hare by name, using an alternative if it was necessary. If they

Above
A hare running down the main street of a village meant that there would soon be a fire

Hares' mantra

It is an old tradition that, on the first day of each month, to protect themselves from evil, superstitious people would recite the words 'Rabbits and Hares' or 'Hares, Hares', before they spoke to anyone else. Sometimes this would even be done when they went to bed the night before

happened to see one on their way to their boats, they would not venture out to sea. Miners too shared the same misgivings.

The three hares motif

A circular design of what looks to be three hares with only one ear each (but giving the impression of two) is wrongly said to be the symbol of local tin miners in the West Country but that is in fact a 20th century myth. The motifs are usually found as medieval roof bosses where the roof is joined to the wall and appear in at least 17 churches in Devon, particularly around Dartmoor. This symbol is known locally but incorrectly as the 'Tinners' rabbits.'

Similar symbols appear in places in England and Wales, France and Germany, as well as in other parts of the world. One (also medieval) appears in a stained glass window in the Holy Trinity church at Long Melford, Suffolk. In China, innumerable

The three hares symbol in the church at South Tawton, Devon. Similar motifs have been discovered across the world but their meaning is not yet understood

(photo by Chris Chapman, The Three Hares Project)

111

seventh century 'Three Hare' or 'Three Rabbit' symbols have been found painted on the ceilings of Buddhist cave temples. They can also be found on fabric, coins, tiles and other objects. It is thought that the hare design may have originated in Persia and from there been spread through its use on precious textiles such as silk which were traded around the world.

Three Hares Project

Dr Tom Greeves MA PhD and his team from the West Country are currently carrying out extensive research into the subject with their 'Three Hares Project'. No one is sure what the symbol actually means but it is thought most likely to be linked to the moon and female fertility as in some of the Devon sites it appears alongside the image of the 'Green Man', the symbol for male fertility. But once again, the hare is the subject of mystery, for not only has this Three Hares symbol appeared across the world for at least 1300 years but more surprisingly it uniquely embraces many different cultures and religions, being found portrayed in Christianity, Islam, Buddhism and Judaism.

Hares and good luck

Despite all these widespread beliefs that the sight of a hare was a bad omen, in a few parts of Britain hares were thought to bring good luck. Some regions held that if a hare was encountered then a wish could be made as soon as it had passed by. To see a black one was a sign of good fortune, although a white one brought bad luck.

Fashionable women used a hare's foot for applying make up and the less privileged as a small brush for dusting little household nooks and crevices. Artists used a hare's foot for painting and taxidermists would smooth down the feathers of their stuffed birds with one. The hair was sometimes used, and still is, for tying artificial flies for fishing. Even today, carrying a hare's foot is considered to bring good luck.

Cultures in the Middle East used the symbol of the hare to signify the good fortune of a great hero. In some ancient Bedouin legends the hare's power to counteract evil forces was specifically identified with the female hare called 'Akrasha.' It

Above
The hare is most often featured on pub signs being chased by hounds, and the pub is invariably called *The Hare and Hounds*. However this pub at Long Melford in Suffolk is just called *The Hare* and the animal is depicted true to life on the sign outside.
A stained glass window in the nearby church of the Holy Trinity depicts a medieval version of the three hares symbol

was believed that she gave protection against leopards and other predators.

Despite its connections with so many unpleasant aspects of life, the hare in many parts of the world was and still is traditionally the symbol of fertility. In India the genitals of a hare were carried to enhance fertility and in ancient Greece, eating the flesh of the hare would make one more sexually attractive.

Not so many years ago, harvesting the last stand of corn in a field was called 'Cutting the Hare'. At one time there had been a country belief that the hare symbolised the 'Corn Spirit' in the crop.

Even today the hare is a popular animal that still holds a place in peoples lives and a few of the traditions and superstitions still survive.

The Leicestershire Hare Pie Scramble

Each year the picturesque village of Hallaton in Leicestershire enacts a centuries old custom called 'The Hare Pie Scramble' by distributing hare pie on Easter Monday. A procession leaves *The Fox* public house in the early afternoon, led by a man dressed in green carrying a pole with a metal hare on the top. Women carrying a basket of bread rolls and a large pie between two of them follow, and behind them walk three men carrying large bottles of beer.

They parade through the village to the cross on the village green, then continue to the church where they stop and throw some pieces of the pie to the crowd. Processing on up the village street they reach the top of Hare Pie Bank where the remaining pie is broken up and thrown to the people gathered there. Then follows a lengthy bottle-kicking match between the locals of Hallaton and the neighbouring village of Medbourne. Springtime hare hunts were once also held at Leicester and at Coleshill in Warwickshire.

Hares in literature

Hares have appeared in literature throughout the centuries, with earliest appearances in Egyptian art and hieroglyphs and then in the Bible. Shakespeare referred more than once to the hare, as

March Hare

'Have some wine,' the March Hare said in an encouraging tone.
Alice looked all round the table, but there was nothing on it but tea.
'I don't see any wine,' she remarked.
'There isn't any,' said the March Hare.
'Then it wasn't very civil of you to offer it,' said Alice angrily.
'It wasn't very civil of you to sit down without being invited,' said the March Hare.

An extract from *Alice's Adventures in Wonderland* by Lewis Carroll

did later poets. More recently it appeared as the Mad March Hare in Lewis Carroll's *Alice's Adventures in Wonderland*. A hare in America is called a rabbit and was the animal from which the character of Bugs Bunny was conceived. It is thought that the tale of Brer Rabbit may have been based on a hare character in a story about an African moon goddess which African slaves brought with them to America.

The Jackalope

It is very doubtful that the white 'Horned hare', or 'Jackalope' – still occasionally found as a stuffed artefact in a glass case in Scotland – ever existed. It is thought most likely to have been a Victorian practical joke. In America it is a hoax that is being perpetuated on websites.

However, in his book *Encyclopaedia of Rural Sports* (1840), Delabere P. Blaine notes that there were accounts of horned hares recorded as early as 1563 by Conrad Gesner, Aldrovandus (d.1605) and many other naturalists. Dr Nehemiah Grew in his *Musaeum Regalis Societatis* (1681) mentions a pair of these hare horns which were at that time in the collection of the Royal Society. In the hands of a skilled taxidermist, a very convincing animal in the form of a white hare with little antlers protruding from the top of its head could well have been concocted.

Another possibility is that American jackrabbits were said to be susceptible to a disease which caused growths on the head and, at a distance, this could be mistaken for little horns. Of course the ears of a hare when pointing forward, could also be mistaken for horns. Interestingly, the Irish word for a 'hare' can also be translated to mean a small deer.

Above
The jackalope, or horned hare, is a fictitious animal which was popular with Victorian taxidermists. It remains a lively myth in the American city of Douglas, Wyoming which calls itself 'Home of the Jackalope'

Proverbs

There are proverbs and sayings still in use today associated with hares. To kiss the hare's foot (meaning to be late) is one of them. To run with the hare and hunt with the hounds describes someone who has double standards and of course there is the uncomplimentary term describing someone as hare-brained, meaning 'scatty' or mad.

The tortoise and the hare

Aesop's fable about the tortoise and the hare is well known. It was observed many years ago that, despite its speed, the erratic behaviour of the hare, involved it running at speed then stopping. Meanwhile a tortoise would get there quicker by steadily trudging on.

Lepus the hare constellation

Hares have always been associated with the darker side of our lives and today in a literal sense they still are, for in the night sky are many groups of stars and there we can find yet another hare. One of these groups is Orion, the Hunter. On his left is Canis Major, his hounds. Due south from the middle of Orion's belt is another constellation called Lepus the Hare which was supposedly killed by Orion.

Below
This Swiss postcard, dated 1900, shows a hare driving a cart-load of Easter eggs and pulled by a snail. It is a curious image which may possibly be inspired by the famous Aesop fable of the hare and the tortoise

Hares and the Law

Legislation regarding hares, and game in general, is a complex subject and some of the current laws date back to the 1830s.

Hares and game birds are deemed to be wild animals and in the *Theft Act 1968* it was stated that wild animals do not belong to anyone. Even so, poaching has always been considered to be an act of theft. In medieval days, hares were considered to be on a par with red deer and wild boar, and were very highly valued for hunting and therefore protected in Britain.

Even up to the early 19th century, poachers were heavily fined, imprisoned or even, in the event of repeated offences, banished to Australia.

Today hares are seldom poached for their meat. Criminal activity relating to a hare is much more likely to be illegal hare coursing, conducted to test dogs against each other and to wager bets of substantial amounts of money on the winner. Illegal hare coursers (those without permission) can be prosecuted under the *Game Act 1831* for trespassing in pursuit of game (poaching)

Above
Hares rely on their speed as a defence. Brown hares can run at up to 45mph (70kph)

117

and not being in possession of a game licence. Hares in this instance are classified as game.

Trapping and netting hares

In the past, many other methods besides dogs were used for poaching. Hares make pathways across fields and through hedges, and these tell-tale routes have always proved useful to either snare or trap hare. Sometimes pit traps called 'hare holes' would be used.

Netting has traditionally been another method of hare trapping and is still used today if it is necessary to catch up hares. 'Long nets', which can be up to 120 yards long and about 4 foot high are supported with stakes 10 yards or so apart. These are placed a few yards out from the edge of a wood or hedge. The hares are then driven towards the nets either by using dogs or by using a cord held between two people which would sweep through the grass or crop where the hares are lying. Shorter nets are used across the gateways which hares often use to escape.

Alternatively, small 'purse nets' can be placed in the runs through a hedge and the hares driven towards these. Other methods of poaching traditionally involved using a stone slinger or catapult, cudgel or a throwstick to kill hares. It is often quite easy to get close to a hare when it is laid low in its form.

Mimicking the call of a leveret in distress can also attract the doe within range. Of course firearms, once they were available to country folk, became yet another way to take hares.

Historic laws

In the late 1300s Richard II imposed a law preventing any layman from keeping greyhounds or using nets or snares to catch hares unless he was a land or property owner, or a senior minister of religion. The less well-paid clergy were barred from hunting hares! Offenders who broke this law could be imprisoned for up to 12 months. In effect this made hunting the hare a privilege of the wealthy.

Henry VIII (in the 1500s) prohibited anyone at all, whatever his position, to use fresh snow to trace or kill a hare. It was quite easy to track a hare in fresh soft snow because the

Below
It is illegal to take or kill a hare on a Sunday or Christmas Day or to offer for sale any British hare or leveret between March and July (inclusive). The Hares Protection Act of 1892 still applies today

In those parts of Britain where the hare is prolific numbers are kept under control by shooting on organised hare drives which take place in February

poor creature would leave a trail and was unable to run as fast as usual in it. There was a hefty fine for anyone caught snow-tracking hares.

Henry VIII enjoyed his fieldsports. In 1536 he issued a proclamation stating his great desire to preserve the pheasants, partridges and hares in his palace grounds from Westminster to St Giles-in-the-Fields, to Islington, Hampstead, Highgate and Hornsey Park. His daughter, Elizabeth I, was also keen on her sport, and is known to have hunted the stag, the fallow deer, the hare and the otter.

As soon as he came on the throne, the sports loving James I fined heavily those who broke the laws protecting hares. If they were unable to pay, then they had to serve six months in gaol. In August 1604 he legislated that only the wealthy could keep greyhounds for coursing hares. Later in the seventeenth century, Charles II brought in further game-protective laws, and in the early 1700s Queen Anne prohibited the netting of hares at night.

Georgian laws to protect the hare

George III brought in further legislation against hare poaching and continued to protect hares by subjecting poachers to a whipping followed by hard labour if they were unable to pay their fine.

He was followed by his son George IV in the 1820s who was even harsher with his punishment of those found guilty of the serial poaching of hares. The first offence merited three

Below
Born to run. In some cases the hare is regarded as game, in others it is classified as a pest

months inside prison, the second offence received six months imprisonment and, if caught for a third time, the offender was put on board a convict ship and sent to Australia for seven years before being allowed to return.

The *Game Act 1831* made it an offence to kill or take a Brown hare on a Sunday or on Christmas day.

In 1815 the St Neots Game Protection Society offered as anti-poaching measures the following rewards for information received concerning poaching incidents:

• Tracing or coursing in the snow £3 3s,

• Killing a leveret in harvest or any other time £2,

• Snaring or night-netting of game £10

• Buying or selling hares or any other game £5.

Many of the old laws mentioned 'hare pipes' as a means of taking hares. What these were is a matter of debate. Some think a hare pipe was a funnel-shaped trap that hares were driven into and caught; while others think a hare pipe was a kind of flute or reed whistle with which the cry of a leveret could be mimicked to attract hares.

Game laws were introduced to protect a landowner's rights to kill or take game and to prevent the unlawful taking or poaching of game.

However, as with so many things to do with hares, there is a grey area. In some cases the hare is regarded as game but in others it is classified as a pest.

Hares only received partial protection when they were included in the *Game Act 1831* which made it an offence to kill or take game on a Sunday or Christmas day. Grouse, black game, pheasants and partridges were all given a close season but not so the hare, even though it had been classified as 'game'.

The *Hares Act 1848* enabled anyone who occupied or owned enclosed land in England or Wales to kill hares without being required to take out a game licence. Another Act in 1860 exempted those pursuing and killing hares by coursing with greyhounds or by hunting with beagles or other hounds from taking out a licence to kill or deal in game.

In 1861 the *Larceny Act* included legislation that dealt with rabbits and hares that were kept in warrens. Any grounds set apart for the breeding of hares or rabbits, whether enclosed or not, constituted a 'warren' within the Act. To take hares or

Below
In the nineteenth century rabbits and hares were sometimes kept commercially in large enclosures or warrens. To take rabbits or hares from a warren became an offence under the *Larceny Act* of 1861. Below, a contemporary rabbit warren in Norfolk

rabbits from a warren was an offence against the Game Laws constituting either trespass in pursuit of game or night poaching, according to the time at which the offence was committed.

Offenders would be tried at quarter sessions or assizes and the crime was punishable by fine or imprisonment.

However, the status of the hare was greatly diminished with the passing of the *Ground Game Act* in 1880. It permitted the occupier of land to kill hares throughout the year, even though he might not have had the right to kill other game. This legislation was blamed by many for the subsequent rapid

Current law

There are restrictions on the killing of hares on moorland and unenclosed (but not arable) land of more than 25 acres between 1 April and 30 June in Scotland and between 1 April and 10 December in England and Wales.

Elsewhere you will not be breaking the law by killing a hare at any time of the year – except on a Sunday or on Christmas day. However they cannot be offered for sale between March and July inclusive.

Legislation in 1948 appeared to override the previous prohibition of shooting hares at night by occupiers or authorised persons. Although under the *Wildlife and Countryside Act 1981* it became illegal to shoot Mountain hares at night with the aid of a lamp or image intensifier or at any time using a semi-automatic weapon. However, under certain circumstances licences could be granted. Night is defined as being from one hour after sunset until one hour before sunrise.

Even though there is no official close season designated for hares, those who course them or hunt with packs of hounds and the vast majority who shoot operate a voluntary close season between March and September. Not so the unregulated poaching gangs.

The official coursing season runs from 15 September to 10 March.

In January 2004, the taking or killing of the Irish hare in Northern Ireland was temporarily prohibited although the ban did not extend to the Brown hare as it is not an indigenous species. Prior to this, hares could only be shot between 12 August and 31 January and could not be taken on Sundays or Christmas day.

decline of hares from an estimated population of four million in the early 1800s. Landowners in some areas became seriously concerned as hare numbers plummeted and their sport declined dramatically, and to remedy this they resorted to purchasing live imported hares from dealers at Leadenhall market, or native ones from gamekeepers on estates where hares were still plentiful.

Some estate owners even set up Hare Preservation Societies which imposed a voluntary close season. However the subsequent *Hares Protection Act 1892* did give hares a little more protection by making it illegal to offer for sale any British hare or leveret in March, April, May, June or July. Neither could hares be taken on Sundays or Christmas Day.

These same laws still apply today.

Below
An unusual photograph showing the incredible endurance of the Brown hare, lying in its form after heavy snow. Henry VIII made it illegal for anyone to use snow as a means of tracking and killing hares

Hare Cookery

The meat of the hare is probably now held at the lowest esteem in Britain that it has ever been. Yet in the late 1800s it was reported that a hare could be bought in Leadenhall market for 5/- (25p) and that hundreds of thousands were eaten each year in Britain. It is no longer highly rated or at least widely served by top chefs and the less privileged majority would sooner buy their dinner in a supermarket than look in the fields for a hare. Hares have a large volume of blood in their bodies which puts many people off eating them and the flesh, unlike rabbit, is dark and has a strong, gamey flavour. It was traditionally taboo for the Celtic people in Britain to eat hare.

Nearly all those killed in Britain today are exported to countries on the Continent, especially France, Germany, Belgium, Holland and Spain, where their meat is still highly regarded. Some of the more eastern European countries are themselves big producers of Brown hares, especially Austria. Competition for sale to the Continent is fierce and challenged by cheap hare meat abundantly produced in Argentina for the European market. The legs and saddles are vacuum packed, frozen and exported to the European market.

Hare recipe books

In a book on hares published in 1903 as part of the *Fur, Feather and Fin* series, recipes for cooking hare are mentioned which were popular as long ago as the reign of Richard II in the late 1300s. One was for 'Harys in Cynee', cynee being a puree of onions slightly thickened with breadcrumbs. 'Harys in Papdele or Padell' was a form of stew served with a stuffing made from the hare's heart, liver and kidneys.

'Harys in Talbotis or Talboytays' was also a sort of stew enriched with the blood as well as spices, seasoning and onions.Hare was also often used for soups when the blood would be included. In 1638 a Doctor Tobias Venner described the flesh of an old hare as being difficult to digest and 'likely to bring on melancholy and cause fearful dreams'.

In the 1800s the hare became classified as game. It was said that a young hare could be selected for roasting or jugging by looking at its claws which should be smooth and sharp and by examining its ears which should be fine and tear easily. Another method used by game dealers to determine the age of a hare was to check the fetlock joint on the front legs. If it was smooth then it was old but if it was knobbly then the hare was a young one. It was a common belief that a hare taken before Christmas was far superior to one after Christmas.

Paunching and hanging a hare

Unlike rabbit, a hare is now thought of as a true game animal and for culinary use is treated very differently to a rabbit. A hare should not be paunched (gutted) until it is prepared for cooking and should be hung up by its back legs in a cool, fly-proof place. A bowl should be placed under its head so that the blood can be collected and saved if required. Two or three drops of vinegar should be added to prevent the blood from congealing. This blood can be used in soup and jugged hare recipes. Cook books

A hare should be hung by its hind legs in a cool fly-proof place and not paunched until it is prepared for cooking

126

often recommend that a hare should be hung for 7 to 10 days but this is entirely a matter of taste. It used to be said that the flesh of a hunted hare was far more tender than one that had been shot. The hunted one could be eaten the same day but the shot one would need hanging for a week.

Preparing a hare for the table

To prepare a hare for the table, it should be laid flat. It is easier to clear up afterwards if it is laid on two or three large sheets of paper. To begin skinning, all four feet should be cut off at the first joint. The belly skin should be cut from between the hind legs up to the chest with a sharp knife or scissors, taking care not to puncture the wall of the abdomen. Then the inside of the hind

'First catch your hare'

In the mid-1700s Hannah Glasse, the 18th century equivalent of Delia Smith, is widely reputed to have written the famous words "First catch your hare". What she actually said was "Take your hare when it is cased" – meaning when it has been skinned. In fact the earliest record of the phrase "First catch your hare" is in 1300 when it was used by Henry de Bracton in *De legibus et consuetudinibus Angliae*

legs should be slit a little way down. As much of the skin as possible should be eased away from the cuts. The hind legs can then be pulled out and the tail cut off. Once this is done it is fairly easy to pull the skin off as far as the head and to ease out the front legs. The head should then be cut off through the neck.

It is only then that the hare should be paunched, by carefully making a slit in the abdomen, taking great care not to puncture the guts inside. The guts and the liver can then be removed easily. The kidneys will be found adhered to the loin and the heart and lungs are behind the diaphragm in the chest cavity and should also be taken out. The heart, liver and kidneys can be saved. If the piece of bone between the hind legs is cut through, the bowel can then be completely removed. Finally the flaps that covered the abdomen should be trimmed off.

The hare can then be jointed by cutting across the spine, immediately in front of the hind legs and again where the ribs begin. This middle joint is called the loin or saddle. The hind legs can then be divided and the front legs cut off. The carcass can quite easily be divided once the flesh has been cut through by dislocating the joints and vertebrae .

Left
Mountain hares feed on natural grasses and heather and are said to have an entirely different flavour to that of a Brown hare

Hare recipes

Hare is most commonly served as soup, a stew, a simple casserole or the gourmet's dish of jugged hare. A full grown hare will serve five or six people. A young one with 'stuffing judiciously flavoured with aromatic herbs, is a dish for the most exacting epicure.' It should have been roasted very slowly and basted and floured frequently. Another culinary recommendation, not likely to find favour today, was to eat a roast hare in perfection – unskinned but with the hair singed or scalded off.

The best flavoured lowland Brown hares are said to come from the Downs and moors rather than arable land because the taste is better if they feed on natural grasses and wild herbs. Mountain or Blue hares are said to have an entirely different flavour to Brown hares, tasting more like grouse with whom they share a similar diet. The Mountain hare was never a popular food with city folk, maybe because, being white, it resembled too closely the domestic cat.

Casseroled saddle of hare served with red currant jelly fresh vegetables, a herb dumpling and a glass of claret

Jugged hare

Perhaps the best known recipe is jugged hare. The hare is prepared by cutting into the joints and by saving the blood. Some recipes recommend that the hare is marinated in wine, herbs and its own blood prior to cooking. Streaky bacon with the rind removed and chopped is fried lightly in a heavy-based pan then some butter is melted in and the joints of hare well browned. Roughly chopped onion, carrots and celery are added, plus some seasoning, a bouquet garni and some finely grated lemon rind.

The whole lot is then covered with stock and brought to the boil in a pan with a tight fitting lid and left to simmer slowly for two to three hours, depending on the size and age of the hare, until the meat is tender. Alternatively it can be put in a heavy oven-proof casserole dish and cooked gently in the oven.

When it is done, the stew is thickened with a little flour and cooked for another minute or two. After being removed from the heat, any blood saved is mixed with some port and added to the stew which should not be reheated afterwards but served immediately with dumplings.

Other traditional accompaniments served with hare are red currant jelly and forcemeat balls.

Perhaps a more appealing recipe (and possibly the original one), with no mention of blood, appeared in *Notes on Game and Game Shooting* by J.J. Manley MA published circa 1880 by the Bazaar Office, London. This recipe said that the hare should be cooked literally in a jug or jar with a loose cover on it. The carcass should be cut into chunks or joints and packed loosely in the jug. A small bunch of sweet herbs, an onion stuck with cloves, a dash of mace and a glass of port wine should be added and topped up with water or stock. The jug should then be put in a slow oven and left to stew gently for three to four hours. The jugged hare should be served hot, accompanied by a sauce of some kind or a few forcemeat balls, according to taste.

Traditionally, hare eaten fresh

In the past when ordinary country people were poor and made the most of a free meal, they usually preferred to have a hare fresh, not hanged, and would soak the joints in milk or cold lightly salted water to draw out the blood and whiten the meat. It was too expensive and time-consuming for them to create the kinds of dishes so loved by gourmets. Haute cuisine and blood were not for them. Besides, most country folk actually liked hares so didn't particularly relish eating them, although this respect may also have had something to do with old taboos. Nevertheless the money they could get from selling a hare, whether poached or obtained legitimately, was usually more useful to them than having it for dinner.

'Jackalope' (sometimes spelt 'Jackaloupe'), the fanciful white-horned hare of Victorian times, still appears on menus in the USA as a dish of thin strips of venison wrapped around a filling of ground roasted rabbit (hare) mixed with spinach and parmesan cheese.

There is insufficient take up from the British public to make it worthwhile for most restaurants to have hare on the menu. One exception is the 18th century Tormaukin Hotel in Glendevon (Scotland) as saddle of hare oven roasted with bacon is served there. Hare is now rarely eaten regularly in the home.

Above
An alternative name for a high hill is a 'Tor' and an old Scottish word for a hare was Maukin. They appear together on this pub sign in Glendevon, Perthshire as 'Tormaukin' which features two Mountain hares with the mountains in the background.

The Name of the Hare

Few animals can have been given as many different names as the hare. Some are very localised and often the hare's alternative names are associated with cats. This is thought to be because both cats and hares have been linked with witches, as their familiars. Another possibility is that a hare has a split upper lip, similar to that of a cat.

In Wales many of the old names for hares include 'cath', which is the word for cat in Welsh. The old Scots word for a Mountain hare was 'malkin' 'mawkin' or 'maukin' but this does not seem to be in use today. However, there is a country inn in Glen Devon called *The Tormaukin* which has a sign depicting two Mountain hares with the mountains in the background. Tor means hill.

In some areas of Scotland, hares are known as 'fite' hares, fite being the word for white in local dialect. The word 'baud' or 'bawd' referred to a hare in Norfolk. 'Wat' or 'watt' is another old

Norfolk name for a hare. Part of the insignia for the town of Watton in Norfolk depicts a hare (or wat) jumping over a 'tun', an old name for a barrel. *The Hare and Barrel* is also the name of a pub in Watton. Shakespeare referred to the hare as a 'wat', a term which has also been used in Cornwall.

Cat and hare names

Some old countrymen in Nottinghamshire would call a hare a 'pussy-bunny' and there were many other nicknames for them which described their habits such as the 'friendless one,' 'furze cat' or 'dew hopper.' An old local Irish name was 'souser'.

The popular hare nicknames used in the past are thought to have been those given to pet cats. Certainly the most common one today still in use, especially by beaglers, is 'puss'. This could also have been derived from Lepus the Latin name for a hare, although the Greeks also referred to a hare as 'puss'.

Traditional names

Other old names still in use today are 'Sally' or 'Owd Sally' or 'Aunt Sally' and 'Sarah' or 'Owd Sarah' or 'Aunt Sarah': also in some areas, 'Molly.' Hares are generally referred to as being female.

Male hares are commonly called 'Jacks' and females 'Jills.'

Right
Many village signs in Norfolk portray local features of interest. This one at Harpley shows pheasants, hares and corn. Place names beginning with 'Har' sometimes indicate a connection with the hare, so the village itself may well have got its name from the abundance of hares that surrounded it

Below left
Hares in England are often called 'puss', perhaps because they have a split upper lip, similar to a cat's

Below
The *Hare and Barrel* pub sign in Norfolk has been cleverly derived from the local town of Watton. 'Wat' was an old name for a hare and 'tun' an old name for a barrel hence Wattun, or as it is now spelt, Watton

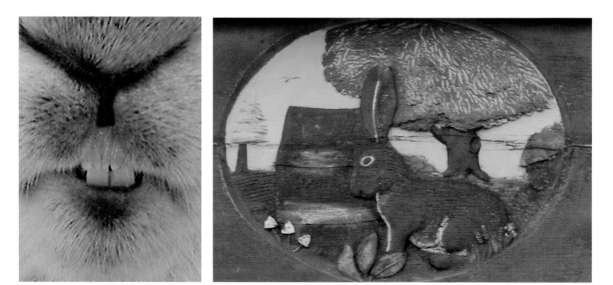

Leverets are sometimes called 'kittens' or 'kindle'. To 'kittle' was to give birth.

The old name for a gathering of hares was a 'husk' or a 'down.'

A 'meuse,' 'smeuse,' 'pad' or a 'smile' was the name given to a pathway (run) regularly used by hares, or for the natural escape route for coursed hares. A 'sough' is an artificial escape hole or refuge created on regularly used coursing grounds such as at Altcar for the Waterloo Cup. The Black Country phrase, 'he's up the sough' (pronounced 'suff') meaning that a man has made himself scarce, is still used today.

A 'smout' or a 'spout' (sometimes also a 'smeuse') described a run made by a hare through the bottom of a wall or beneath a hedge.

A 'wrench' is the term used when a hare makes a sharp right-angled turn when being coursed.

A 'form,' 'seat' or 'couch' is the place where a hare settles in and lies low during the daytime. It is a shallow depression pressed down in the earth or vegetation.

Below
The Hare family have been landowners in Norfolk for centuries and have had connections with the village of Stow Bardolph since 1553. This carving of a hare on one of the choir stalls represents the Hare family in Holy Trinity church

From the north to south and east to west of England, there are a number of places that include hares in their name: in Yorkshire there is Harehills, Hampshire has Harestock; in Gloucestershire there is Haresfield. Hare Green and Hare Street are both in Essex. There is another Hare Street in Hertfordshire. Harehope is in Northumberland, a county that is still a stronghold of the hare and where packs of beagles visit to hunt by invitation. Perhaps at one time hares even boxed at Harefield in Greater London. The names of many other places that begin with 'Har' may also indicate a past connection with hares.

Left
'Return from the hunt,' an Egyptian painting dating from 1,500 BC. Hares have been hunted for many centuries all over the world

The Hare and Fieldsports

Hares have probably been prized even more for the sport they offer than for their culinary potential. Murals show that the ancient Egyptians used running dogs to hunt hares. The fact that coursing has been popular for more than 30 centuries is borne out by many ancient drawings and carvings. At least one Chinese emperor, Kamhi, is recorded as having hunted hares with greyhounds.

The chase of the hare was prevalent throughout eastern Europe long before it became a favourite pastime in Britain. It is commonly held that the Romans introduced the Brown hare to Britain, and certainly they greatly appreciated hares for their sporting potential. Caesar is said to have remarked on the fact that the Britons did not eat the flesh of the hare, even though the animal was plentiful. It was probably the Mountain hare that he was commenting about, an animal sacred to the Celts.

From the thirteenth century until today, the Brown hare has been conserved in England for the pleasure of hunting them.

A pack of beagles are always hunted on foot, as opposed to harriers which are hunted on horseback

135

King John obviously enjoyed his sport in the thirteenth century because he regularly received greyhounds in lieu of money for fines, grants or forfeits. One such fine paid in 1203 was said to be 500 merks, 10 horses and 10 leashes (hunting pairs) of greyhounds. Another lesser debt was settled in 1210 with one swift-running horse and six greyhounds.

At this time, a special kind of greyhound (termed Leporarii) was kept in England and France. King John kept a kennel of this breed of dogs in Cumberland.

Hare Coursing

Coursing is thought to have originated among the Celtic Gauls in France. They are said to have employed hare finders to beat the cover. When the hare was put up, a man on foot would unleash the greyhounds, while a single horseman would keep up with them. This is broadly the same as open coursing today.

Other animals such as deer and fox were also sometimes coursed. In time it became a favourite pastime in Britain, and in Wales, coursing was called 'helfa a dolef' which means the shouting chase because of the noise made by the sportsmen.

In the mid-1800s, the principal coursing meetings were held at Altcar, Ashdown Park and Stonehenge. It was a very popular

True sportsman

In 125 AD the Roman author Flavius Arrianus (Arrian) wrote in his book *On Hunting Hares*:

"The true sportsman does not take out his dogs to destroy hares but for the sake of the course and the contest between the dogs and the hares and is glad if the hare escapes."

Below
Spectators and a bookie at an official coursing meeting in 2004

sport amongst the pitmen who worked in the coal mines. At places like Carmichael in Lanarkshire and Bothal in Northumberland, their greyhounds could hold their own against those owned by the wealthy, for even then it was a sport in which anyone could compete regardless of their status, just as it is today.

By the late 1800s coursing was a major sport and huge crowds were attracted to meetings all over the UK. Carrier pigeons were used to take the results to all the major cities and it was said that the London Stock Exchange closed early when the news of the winners of the biggest meeting began to arrive.

At an official coursing meeting two dogs are run against each other. The hare is given a lead of about 100 yards before the pair are released by a slipper. The dogs are distinguished by wearing a red or white collar, the one with the white collar is held on the slipper's right

Not seen for nearly 100 years: Enclosed or Park coursing

Some private coursing meetings were held on 'enclosed' land which meant the ground was surrounded by high walls, fences or thick hedges with little gaps left in them through which the hare could escape from the dogs. Often the hares would have been caught up from the wild. Enclosed coursing meetings flourished towards the end of the 1800s. Haydock and Gosforth Park near Newcastle upon Tyne were favoured venues but the enclosed (park) coursing did not remain popular and the coursing grounds mentioned eventually became racecourses for horses. There has been no enclosed coursing in England since 1914 and it has since been prohibited by the National Coursing Club.

In all official events now the hares live completely wild and naturally until the day they are coursed.

Irish hares were imported at one time for coursing as it was believed that they were fitter and stronger. Ironically, at about the same time, Brown hares were being taken to Ireland for the same reason.

The first official British coursing club was the Swaffham Coursing Society in Norfolk which was founded by Lord Orford in 1776 and is still operating today.

The National Coursing Club has strict control over all public coursing meetings.

At present there are 23 registered Greyhound Hare Coursing clubs in England.The first official greyhound stud book was begun in 1882.

The Waterloo Cup is the ultimate coursing prize. The meeting was first held at Altcar in Lancashire in 1836 and continues to be held at the end of February each year.

Above
Hare coursing with grey hounds has been a popular sport for centuries.
Banning hare coursing would have an adverse effect on the hare population in England. Estates that now preserve the hare for official coursing meetings would probably strictly control their numbers so as not to attract the attention of illegal hare coursers who would continue to disregard the law just as they do already

Left
The Judge mounted on horseback at an official coursing meeting awards points to the dogs

The Rules of Hare Coursing

A greyhound can run faster than a hare, but at official driven coursing meetings it is a requirement that the hare must be given a 100-yard headstart (known as 'the law') before the dogs are released. Two greyhounds are run off against each other on a knock-out basis. The man holding the greyhounds is referred to as a 'slipper' and he waits, hidden from view, behind what is called a 'shy' until the beaters drive a hare past him. A hare can run up to 45 mph and a greyhound can achieve an initial speed of 55 mph over a short distance.

Within a few hundred yards the dogs catch up with the hare but by then they will have slowed down to about 40 mph. Having all-round vision and good hearing, the hare is well aware of their position and at the crucial moment jinks sharply away from them causing the greyhounds to momentarily lose sight of their quarry and to over-run. This may happen several times but the dogs tire quickly and the hare, having the better stamina, more often than not gets away.

The sole aim of hare coursing is to see which dog 'turns' the hare most often. It is rare for a healthy hare to be killed and if one is, the slipper will consider increasing the head start for the next hare

Greyhounds usually try to run alongside the hare and lower their heads to grab hold of it but if they learn to tip it over from behind then they are more likely to catch it. Once the hare has been lost from sight, the greyhounds give up the chase.

They are awarded points for reaching the hare first and then for turning it by a judge mounted on horseback but receive no extra points if they catch one. The greyhounds wear either a white collar or a red one and the judge identifies the winner by holding up an appropriately coloured handkerchief.

Sometimes a 'bye' is run with only one dog. It is done out of fairness if the opposing dog has been withdrawn for some reason. This means that the dog left in the competition undertakes the same number of runs as its future opponents. It is surprising that sometimes more hares are caught in this situation than when two dogs are run together. As the dog is on its own it can concentrate entirely on the hare without having to consider the other competing greyhound.

Walked-up hares

Some meetings are held in which hares are walked up rather than driven. A few people spread out across a field and begin to

Coursing USA

In the United States coursing hares became a very popular sport after the Civil War. Indeed it has been popular for centuries in cultures as diverse as China, France and Syria

Left
The saluki is an ancient breed from Arabia used by the nomadic Bedouin tribesman for hunting. Those used for coursing in England are lighter framed than the show specimens

walk through the cover. A 'slipper' holds the two dogs whose turn it is to run: when a hare is flushed, it is given at least a hundred-yard lead before the dogs are released.

Coursing Dogs

Long dogs

Deerhounds are large dogs and several meetings are organised specially for them each year.

Salukis, the equivalent of the British greyhound in Arabian countries, have been very highly valued in the Middle East for centuries. A skeleton with bone structure identical to that of a saluki was found in Syria and has been identified as being 4,000 years old. The nomadic Bedouin tribes hunted not only hares with their sight hounds but also gazelle and the desert oryx. Salukis are renowned for their endurance as well as their speed. Today, because of diminishing wildlife, hunting with salukis is restricted in many Arab countries but this age-old tradition is still cherished and practiced where possible. In Britain there are several coursing clubs for salukis. Like the desert salukis, these dogs are lighter-framed than those which represent the breed in the show ring.

Many Welsh and English coal miners used to keep whippets for racing and coursing hares. A whippet can reach a speed of 35mph and a skeleton closely resembling one was discovered at Avebury in Wiltshire, the bones of which were identified as being 4,500 years old.

These breeds, along with greyhounds, are called long dogs, sight hounds or gaze hounds and they hunt purely by sight, losing interest once their quarry disappears from view.

Lurchers

Lurchers, however, are used to course hares both officially and unofficially, legally and illegally. Lurchers are of mixed breeding with greyhound, whippet, saluki or deerhound blood, quite often with a dash of Bedlington terrier or collie. This mix can produce a dog that not only hunts by sight but also uses its nose and is often very intelligent and possesses stamina. Used during

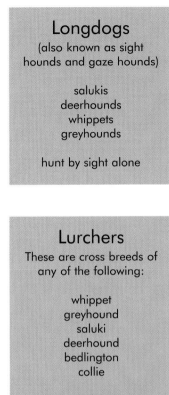

Longdogs
(also known as sight hounds and gaze hounds)

salukis
deerhounds
whippets
greyhounds

hunt by sight alone

Lurchers
These are cross breeds of any of the following:

whippet
greyhound
saluki
deerhound
bedlington
collie

hunt by sight and scent

Lurchers are dogs of mixed breeding used to course hares officially, unofficially and sometimes illegally

the night as well as daytime, some are trained to run down the beam of a lamp focused on the quarry that might well be a fox or a rabbit instead of a hare.

Organised lurcher coursing meetings take place under National Coursing Club rules with its own strict code of conduct. The dogs may be run in pairs or sometimes singly.

Coursing meetings today are social events where like-minded people gather to enjoy each other's company and to see who owns or has trained the best dog.

The coursing season

There are official coursing clubs throughout the country and the season runs from 15 September to 10 March, with the major meeting held at Altcar at the end of February each year. Remarkably in the 1870s, well before the invention of the motor car, the spectacle of watching top class greyhounds at Altcar drew crowds as big as 80,000. Nowadays the Waterloo Cup is attended by up to 12,000 spectators as well as scores of anti-coursing protesters. The phenomenal interest in coursing live hares began to wane when track racing over set distances and using an artificial hare came into being in 1926.

Irish Hare Coursing

In Ireland there is very little official walked-up coursing. Some open coursing meetings are held but 'park' or 'enclosed' coursing is also popular.

The rules for official park coursing in Ireland are somewhat different to those on the British mainland. Meetings are held in an area possibly as large as 200 metres wide by 500 metres long, fenced round with netting the end part of which is raised sufficiently for the hare to escape beneath it from the dogs and run into another paddock.

Straw bales protect the dogs from the fences when the hare disappears. Unlike the 'open' coursing practiced in Britain where Brown hares are driven off open fields onto the coursing ground, the native Irish hares are first caught from the wild in different areas by driving them into a catching net. They are

The Moocher

The moocher (*above*) is the ultimate all-round lurcher, one that is worked by itself. It finds its own quarry, it will chase anything, fur or feather, day or night and the best are trained to retrieve to hand. In the past, lurchers had a reputation for being the poachers' dog as indeed they mostly were. They were said to have got their name from the Romany word 'lur' meaning 'thief'. However, in the last few years they have become increasingly popular not only for hunting but also as pets and there are more than 50 local clubs, most of which are affiliated to the officially-recognised Association of Lurcher Clubs

then taken to the coursing ground and released into a large paddock of maybe three or four acres in size where they are held for two or three weeks before the meeting. During this time they receive additional food in the way of rolled oats and pellets and are trained by driving them into a small holding pen from where they are run down the course so that they become familiar with the escape routes. Depending on the size of the meeting, up to a hundred hares may be gathered together.

When the actual coursing meeting takes place all the greyhounds are muzzled. It is only since the 1990s that muzzling has been compulsory. The hare is given a lead (a law) of about 100 yards before the two dogs are slipped. The dog that reaches the hare first scores the majority of points with additional points being scored for each time the hare is turned.

After the hares have been coursed they are caught up from the holding paddock and returned to the wild. Special release areas are chosen where they are most likely to thrive. The hares are not always freed back in the same place as they were caught, not a bad thing because it introduces fresh blood into a region.

Above
The beagle. Elizabeth I was said to have kept a pack of 'pocket' beagles, less than ten inches high at the shoulders. Charles II is also known to have hunted with beagles

Self-interest to protect the hare

Members of Irish coursing clubs conserve hares in the wild by managing habitat and controlling predators during the main breeding season. It is in their own interest to ensure that the hares are properly cared for. Because the people involved in coursing catch up and handle the hares, they are able to supply samples and DNA material from the hares for researchers to help them in their work. Using this 'park' method of coursing has very little impact on the hare population, as very few die, although it is inevitable that there will be the occasional injury.

In one survey in Northern Ireland, reported on TV, six hares were tagged that had been netted, penned and then coursed and subsequently released. It was found that none of them suffered any ill effects and when returned to their previous environment, had survived and bred.

However on mainland Britain where the hares are coursed a longer distance on open fields, it was found that there were more injuries to hares if the greyhounds were muzzled.

Below
The harrier. It is recorded that Xenophon (435-354 BC), the Greek soldier and historian who wrote essays on horsemanship, hunting and cavalry warfare, used harriers to catch hares

Hunting for Hares

Three types of hounds are used in packs to hunt hares, mainly the Brown hare. In 2004 there were 69 beagle, 21 harrier and 11 basset packs officially registered in England and Wales. In Northern Ireland there were three beagle packs, 17 foot harrier packs and 10 mounted harrier packs hunting Irish hares, as well as other packs kept in Eire.

Left
Small hunting dogs the size of the beagle were recorded 2,400 years ago in ancient Greece

The beagle

The Beagle stands about 15 inches at the shoulder and is hunted by people on foot. It is sometimes called a 'jelly dog' because red currant jelly is often served with the hare it hunts! It is only during the last century that beagles have become standardised as a type but they are thought to be the oldest of pure-bred British hounds. One theory is that they got the name 'beagle' from the Celtic word 'Baeg' meaning small but others believe the breed originated in Greece. Certainly small hunting dogs were recorded there as long ago as 400BC.

Queen's favourite

Basset hounds were a favourite of Queen Alexandra who kept several in her kennels. The name basset is said to have evolved from the French word 'Bas' meaning low

The harrier

The Harrier is a larger dog, standing at about 18 inches at the shoulder and has probably had an infusion of foxhound blood

144

at some time. These are hunted and followed on horseback.

In 1830 a pack of harrier hounds were kept at Garella, near St Petersburg, by British residents in Russia. At that time a writer in *The Sporting Magazine* reported that the pack with mounted followers rode out for about five miles, whereupon the hounds were 'thrown' into some low brushwood. They soon found a hare that went away as straight as any dog fox. It was also noted that there were two kinds of hares in that area of Russian plains, the common Brown hare and a lighter grey hare which turned white in winter and was said to always run straight and not double back like the Brown. The same pack of hounds was also used to hunt wolf and fox.

There were many private packs kept in the 19th century. The oldest English pack dates back to 1745 and the Welsh Anglesey Harriers could trace their beginnings back to 1744. The hounds used to hunt hares are now recorded in the Masters of Harriers and Beagles Association Stud Book. Harriers will also sometimes be used to hunt foxes.

The basset

Bassets, like beagles, are hunted on foot. The basset is a slower dog, longer in the body than a beagle, with shorter legs in

The Easton Harriers move off from the meet. A pack of harriers is used to hunt hares from horseback

Harrier history

The name harrier is thought to have derived from a Norman-Saxon word meaning a general working dog and was used collectively until the 18th century. Harriers have been known in Britain since the Middle Ages and it is possible that they were introduced here by the Romans. The modern breed standard was first identified in the late 18th century

Left
A meet of the Wiltshire and Infantry Beagles. Many packs of beagles were originally associated with schools, colleges or army regiments

relation to its body. It is also heavier although the type used for hunting is lighter-framed than those seen in the show ring. The pack's pattern of hunting is to follow one another rather than spreading out and working individually. The breed originated in the 15th century and was imported into Britain, most probably from France, by either Lord Galway in 1866 or Everett Millais in the 1870s. Both have been credited with their introduction.

Pack requisites

Hounds are counted in 'couples' and typically a pack kept for hunting hares will consist of 12-20 couples ie 24 to 40 hounds. To be successful, a pack of hounds requires team-work during which individual hounds with different attributes combine to work together and complement each other. To amalgamate and form an efficient pack, the qualities needed are a good voice, good nose, stamina, pace, drive and perseverance. A pack may cover a distance of 20-30 miles in a day.

Hunting the hare does not receive the publicity that fox hunting does but nevertheless it has a band of dedicated followers. A hundred years ago there were 119 packs of harriers and 48 packs of beagles. Today there are about 100 registered packs of hounds that specifically hunt hares. Beagles, which are hunted on foot, are now in the majority. There are also a few packs of

Izaak Walton

As the Hunter says, "You know there is more sport in hunting the hare than in eating of her."

The Compleat Angler, 1653

basset hounds that, like beagles, are hunted on foot. Some beagle packs were kept privately while others were originally associated with schools, colleges and army regiments. As a general rule, beagle packs usually now meet on Wednesdays and Saturdays, most often after midday which once fitted in with the times allocated for sports for students and officers, and was also early closing day for shops!

Hunt followers

People from all walks of life take great pleasure in watching harriers or beagles working, even though few hares are killed. On average probably only one hare is killed for every other outing where they are plentiful, far fewer in other places.

A hare in its prime and fully fit is unlikely to be caught. Those killed are usually in some way sick or injured, many previously maimed by road traffic and farm machinery. Hounds administer a far quicker death than a lingering one through sickness or injury. The followers take most pleasure from being out in the countryside, getting some exercise, watching the wildlife around them, seeing hounds work and not knowing what is going to happen next. Nearly all of them will say they have had a great day out if the hound work has been good, even if there has not been a kill. Hoping for a kill is not the reason that most followers go out.

Scent

There is no doubt that a hare is aware of the scent it leaves behind and a predator's ability to follow it. Scent can vary greatly depending on weather conditions and the vegetation but the science of scent remains a mystery. It is better on damp days and often on days when the ground is warmer than the air. It can be strong on grass or young corn but almost non-existent on plough.

When it is good, hounds will work quickly on a line but when it is bad they have to keep checking and spreading out to search for a clue. If the hounds are unable to pick up a line, their huntsman will cast them out in ever greater circles around where they have lost it in an effort to help them find it again.

Secrets of scent

Scent is better on damp days, especially when the ground is warmer than the air. Scent can be strong on grass or young corn but almost non-existent on plough (*below*)

The cunning hare

The hare's is cunning and uses many tricks to throw the hounds off its line, such as running along the top of a wall, back tracking, making a big leap or crossing a river. A hare will suddenly clap down so that a pack of hounds will run over it or push a fresh hare out of its form to take over the running. On a day when scent is really bad, beagles have been seen standing on top of the hare they are hunting without realising it is there.

One account records how a second hare ran alongside the pack, then veered in between them and the hunted one, so that the hounds took up the fresh line, allowing the tired one to escape. Although they do not normally go to ground it is not uncommon for a hunted hare to take refuge in a rabbit hole, buildings, a drain or a stack of bales.

Behaviour of the hunted hare

Hares do not like running directly into a strong wind and a hunted hare normally prefers to run down-wind because not only does it rely on its eyes to locate its pursuer, but it also has acute hearing and listens to any noises coming from behind it. If closely observed, the ears can be seen moving in an effort to pick up every sound.

Hares also find it advantageous to run uphill whenever possible because of their long back legs. When there is a covering of light snow or in icy conditions the hare has an advantage over the chasing dog because its feet are covered in fur and it can get a better grip on the slippery ground than the dog with its bare pads. A tired hunted hare will usually run with its hindquarters higher than usual.

Most hares run in a very large sweeping circle covering several large fields and an area of up to two square miles. A notable hunt may last for a couple of hours with hounds running one hare the whole time. If, as rarely happens, the hare decides to go straight it may take the hounds as far as five miles. This occasionally happens after Christmas and is normally a jack hare which has come well out of its normal range in search of a female. Beaglers call this a 'Straight-neck Jack'. Too many hares in an area will spoil a hunt because hounds switch from one to

Above
A beagle huntsman in the distinctive green and white livery

The hare hunting season

The hare hunting season is from about the middle of September when all the corn has been cut until the end of March. Early morning or late afternoon meets are held at the beginning of the season to get young hounds acquainted with the job and old hounds fit. The opening meet after which serious hunting begins is usually some time during the first two weeks in October

another denying the followers the pleasure of watching the skill and tenacity the pack need to come to terms with a hare.

How the hunt is conducted

It is the huntsman who carries the horn and is responsible for working the hounds. He begins a hunt by working them across a field in search of a hare. The hounds may either happen across one in its form, or find one by picking up and working on an old scent line. The masters and whippers-in (assistants) spread out across the surrounding fields from where the hounds are being worked. They usually try to get on high ground from where they can see what is happening and be prepared to turn the pack away from busy roads or places they are not allowed to go. They are there to assist the huntsman and between them keep in touch with the pack.

The traditional dress for beagling officials consists of a green jacket and white breeches, but the running shoes need to be comfortable at all costs and their style varies. A pack of beagles in full cry move quickly and the people working them need to be able to cover the ground with equal speed.

In Continental Europe, it is customary for only a few hounds to be used and these are changed with fresh ones during the hunting day. They are most often used to find and then push hares out of the cover towards waiting guns. A similar method

Hare hunting statistics

About 1,500 hares a year are accounted for by hunting in Britain. The usual quarry is the Brown hare. Mountain hares are seldom hunted. In Ireland the Irish hare is also hunted with packs of beagles and harriers. In the late 1800s some Irish hares were imported to Yorkshire for hunting with harriers

Keepers and their helpers on the annual hare shoot on an estate in Norfolk. This is 'walked-up' shooting in which the guns progress in a line through the fields, putting up the hares as they disturb them

of hunting is used for wild boar and fox. Continental hare hunts are often conducted with a great deal of ceremony, with a fanfare on a French horn before and after the hunt. Hounds may also be blessed by a priest at the meet.

Shooting the Hare

In the 16th and 17th century, firearms were sufficiently reliable to be used in the chase and they completely superseded the long bow and cross bow which had been used by hunters for centuries.

Prolific bags of the past

The Brown hare must have once been very common across Europe. On the Continent, phenomenally large bags have been recorded in the past. When in the early 1800s the 'battue' (the wholesale slaughter of game) was fashionable in Germany, a shooting party bagged 2,400 hares in four days on the rich plains near Magdeburg. As long ago as 1753, bags of 2,000 a day were being recorded in Bohemia and Austria. At Chantilly in France between 1748 and 1779, a total of 77,150 hares were bagged. In 1889 Prince Phillipe de Caraman-Chimay shot 8,000 in five days and Prince Lichtenstein accounted for 2,540 in two days. On the estate of the Archduke Frederic Belize, nearly 33,000 hares were killed in 1905.

Even though British records for brown hares don't match these astronomical figures, some large bags have been achieved in the past revealing just how abundant the Brown hare must have been in England. In 1806 on the manor of Sir Thomas Gooch, 6,000 hares were killed. Perhaps the most consistent of all was Holkham Estate in North Norfolk. Their record was reached on 19th December 1877 when 11 guns shot 1,215 hares. Over 1,000 had already been shot only five days previously. Other big bags had been achieved on the estate on January 1st 1856 with 1,056, in December 1857 with 1,146 and in December 1860 with 1,153. Following the record day in 1877, a bag of over 1,000 was shot in December 1881.

Another Norfolk estate to have a large population of hares

2nd Marquess of Ripon

One of the most famous of all the Victorian shots was the 2nd Marquess of Ripon whose personal record for number of hares shot in one season stood at 2,152 in 1878 (although these were not necessarily all shot in Britain). During his shooting 'career' between 1867 and the outbreak of World War I he accounted for more than 30,000 hares to his own gun

was Gunton where on 3rd December 1875 eight guns shot 614 hares. On 17th November 1881 a mixed bag of 733, which included 257 hares, was shot out of the 13 acre Antingham wood. At that time the policy for game management on the estate required that the keepers culled Jack hares in February and March, being paid 1/- a head for doing so. In some years 400 would be culled in this way.

Across the country, bags of more than 500 hares were not unusual. Records show this happened in Yorkshire, Nottinghamshire and the north of Cumbria. In Wiltshire, which is still a stronghold of the Brown hare, a total of just over 3,000 were shot on one estate in the 1869/70 season and at Cheveley Park near Newmarket 2,442 hares were taken in the 1894/5 season.

While these are record bags, the estates in question consistently shot large numbers over the years. Hare shooting was obviously a very popular sport among the gentry in those days. Even today some of the big estates in the most favoured areas will cull up to 500 hares in a day during their annual February hare shoot. Shooting Mountain/Blue hares in Scotland was also popular in Victorian times and it was common for parties to ride out on ponies, even a distance of seven miles from the shooting lodge, to shoot driven Mountain hares. One report from the Grampians records 715 being shot in this manner. In November

Plans to double hare numbers by 2010

The EU requires member states under its Bio-diversity Action Plan (BAP) to help certain key species. It is hoped to double Brown hare numbers by 2010. However in some areas of Britain such as East Anglia numbers are already so high that an annual cull is necessary

1889 at Logiealmond (Perthshire) six guns shot 1,289 hares in one day and in October 1896 1,100 were shot at Loch Ericht and 900 at Dunalastair. Later on in December 1922 at Glen Dye, 1,204 were accounted for in one day and nearly 7,000 were killed that year.

In the late 1920s it was not unusual for a shooting party to bag 1,000 Mountain hares a day in the Highlands. However it did not profit the estate owners for what they got paid for a dead hare failed to cover the cost of getting it to market, let alone the cost of the ammunition used to shoot it. It was also said that the pelts of the young ones were so tender and fragile that the furriers could not use them and therefore was of no value either.

Organised hare shoots

Today, hare shooting as a sport does not appeal to most British sportsmen. However many Europeans greatly enjoy shooting hares, as do many in the USA.

Many overseas visitors will pay for a day's organised hare shooting in Britain if they have the opportunity. The Italians in particular very much enjoy the sport and for example each year up to 70 of them share a day on a well-known Norfolk estate. They are divided into two groups, both of whom carry shotguns. One team stands forward while the other walk the hares towards them. On the next drive the team that has been walking changes over with the ones who have stood. For safety's sake the team walking are only allowed to shoot hares going forward until they reach a certain point at a safe distance from the standing guns, at which time a whistle is blown and they have to cease shooting.

Hares that are shot by the walking guns are collected up behind the line by a keeper on a quad bike. The total bag is usually between three and four hundred.

Elsewhere in the UK days are taken by groups of Greeks, and Germans and the Belgians visit Scotland to shoot Mountain hares. The latter prefer to stand only and have hares driven towards them. This is obviously more expensive as beaters have to be paid for. Income for the estate is obtained not only from letting the shooting but also from the sale of the hares, most of which the overseas visitors themselves take home. Hare shooting is some countries such as Hungary, Austria and Germany has become almost a religion involving much ceremony and is often followed by a party afterwards. In Europe the meat of a hare is rated as a delicacy.

In some parts of Europe, particularly Scandinavia, hares are not driven towards standing guns. Instead it is a somewhat solitary sport with one or two people going out with a hound-like dog that they hope will be able to locate a hare by scent. As hares

There is a strong theme in German children's literature which shows the hare turning the tables on the hunter. This is a particularly ferocious example!

On the driven shoot, beaters are used to drive hares towards the guns. They are also used to drive the hares towards the running ground for coursing

usually tend to run in a very large circle, the guns try to position themselves where they think the hare will come past them when the dog has rousted it. A tracking device is often attached to a collar on the dog as hares are not only hunted in the open ground but also in woodland.

Sometimes the Russians use shotguns to shoot Mountain hares in the snow, riding pillion on ski-doos (a cross between a sled and a motor bike) travelling at 20 to 30 mph. Game of any species in Russia is carefully monitored and bag limits decided according to the season. The hare shooting season is from September until the end of February.

Brown hare culls

Hare shooting in Britain is generally arranged as being a means of controlling numbers where there are too many, especially in counties such as Norfolk and Berkshire. Where there is a big population, this is done by way of organised hare drives and shooting them with shotguns. There is always the risk of a hare going away wounded using any method of shooting but providing experienced guns are doing the job then this risk is kept to a minimum.

While those asked on a hare shoot enjoy the opportunity of meeting up with other people and taking some sporting shots, many of them do not relish the fact that it is the hare that is the quarry. However, thinning their numbers out is a job that needs to be done for the general well-being of both the hare population and the farmer's crops. Providing the hares are shot at when they are well within range, they are not a difficult target for they are large animals and quite often not fast-moving when they come forward. Those being driven are more aware of what is happening behind them than looking for danger in front of them. Several Norfolk estates kill 400 or more in a day on their annual hare drive, taking in an area of 2,000 or 3,000 acres. Even so there will be plenty of hares left on pieces of ground that aren't included in the drives or those that get away.

Brown hares are usually culled during the first two weeks of February when the game shooting season is over and before breeding gets fully under-way. It is a necessary operation for the

Above
When not hard-pressed, hares will stop and sit up to look around – this behaviour can make them an easy target for a gun. Hare shooting as a sport does not appeal to most British sportsmen

Not so rare at night

Even in their regional strongholds, hares only appear abundant to the casual observer in the Spring. After that they seem to disappear. However, shine a light round the fields at night, at any time of year, and it will be seen just how plentiful is the hare

interest of the farmer, the forester and the hare. A team of forty or more people armed with shotguns surround a large area of ground and drive the hares towards a line of people standing who are also armed with guns. Only hares going back are shot at by the walking guns. Hares are very heavy to carry and it is a foolish beater who shoots more than the odd one, for he probably has a long way to carry them to the end of the drive. It is the standing guns in front who shoot the majority of the hares.

In general, on formal driven shoots for pheasants and partridges, the rule is that no ground game (hares and rabbits) should be shot. This isn't always the case. One person who knew only too well the weight of three hares was loading for his employer, a Lord, who was a walking gun alongside a wood on a pheasant drive. Being allowed to shoot ground game, his Lordship had already shot two hares that his loader was obliged to carry when he put his gun up to a third. His loader immediately shouted that it was too far. This put his Lordship off and he didn't fire his gun. Turning to his man he said, 'George, that hare wasn't out of shot,' to which George promptly replied, 'I know Mi-lord but it was too far for me to carry it!'

Cull figures

The annual hare cull figures on one large Norfolk estate have been recorded as follows:

2002 total 1,006 culled

2003 total 917 culled

2004 total 1,673 culled

On this estate, annual culls have exceeded 1000 on many occasions in the last 150 years.
The consistency of these figures shows that properly managing the population of Brown hares by shooting is in no way detrimental to numbers. The remaining hares have more food and better health.

Fifty per cent hare culls

It is estimated that over 50% of the hare population is killed in the area of a hare shoot but this number can be quickly compensated for by way of less competition for food which results in bigger litters being born. Culling also reduces hare disease. It is difficult for people to imagine that 50% culls are justifiable if they live in areas where the sight of a Brown hare is a rarity. Even when driving round the hare's stronghold in Norfolk during daytime, the hare doesn't seem to be common enough to warrant those sort of figures, for very few are likely to be seen unless it is in the Spring. After that they seem to disappear. However, shine a light round the fields at night, any time of year, and it will be seen just how plentiful is the hare.

Shooting is an efficient way of reducing numbers but it is not selective. In coursing or hunting it is normally the hares that are not fully fit for some reason or other that get caught. It is extremely rare for one to get away injured.

Lamping at night with either a shotgun or a .22 rifle is another legal method by which numbers can be reduced. It is often used where there are insufficient hares to justify a driven shoot.

Illegal Hare Coursing

Most landowners are willing to accommodate hares but not the undesirable characters who seek to pay them a visit. Therefore many estates shoot hares by lamping in order to keep hare numbers down so that they don't attract the attentions of illegal coursers. This sadly is the case in many parts of the country and is no doubt partly responsible for the decline in hare numbers.

These illegal hare coursers have no respect for the hare: in fact they frequently throw the carcass in a ditch after their dogs have caught one. Not only that but they drive vehicles across crops and through hedges and fences, as well as often taking the opportunity to look around for anything worth stealing.

If they are accosted they can be very abusive and threatening and have been known to retaliate by returning to set fire to stacks and barns.

The rural crimes these people commit are very difficult to deal with and sadly it is the hare that has to pay the ultimate price.

Mountain Hare Shoots

Shooting of Mountain hares today is mainly to reduce numbers where they have become excessive. Large numbers can damage the heather giving it little chance to regenerate and hares also act as host to ticks, spreading disease among sheep and grouse.

Also if they are present where attempts are being made to establish woodland, they can soon decimate the newly-planted trees.

A few Mountain hare shoots are let to overseas visitors, usually the French, Belgian and Italians. In Scotland it is the keepers and their helpers who shoot on the whole. This is usually arranged after the grouse shooting finishes in mid-December. The hares are driven with a team of beaters past a line of grouse butts or over a ridge where the standing guns are

Above
The Mountain hare can decimate newly-planted woodland

waiting. The hares tend to favour running on patches of frozen snow rather than through the vegetation. Bags of 200 to 300 in a day can be achieved in this way.

Falconry

Falconry is an ancient sport and is still practiced by a few enthusiasts today. Game birds and rabbits are the usual quarry but the larger birds of prey such as the Red-tailed hawk and Goshawk are capable of catching and despatching a hare.

However, because the hare is such a strong animal, the hawk is very much in danger of being injured or having its feathers damaged and it is not a risk all falconers wish to take.

A mature goshawk 'mantles' over its kill - the typical protective gesture of the raptor, designed to hide the prey from the attention of other hawks *(photo courtesy of David Kjaer)*

A Future for the Hare

The Brown hare has suffered a substantial decline since the middle of the last century. It is estimated that the present population of Brown hares is between 800,000 and one million.

For monitoring purposes, attempts are made to count hares in the spring but it is very difficult to do because of the creature's nocturnal habits and its highly effective camouflage. One way this can be done is to search one kilometre squares by walking diagonally across them and counting the hares that are flushed. An alternative method is known as 'night driven transects' which involves lamping the hares after dark with a million-candle power spotlight from a slow-moving vehicle across a fixed area over a period of several nights. The count is probably more accurate by this method. Thermal imaging and night vision equipment can play an increasingly important part in studying such a nocturnal animal.

Researchers also rely on records kept by the official coursing societies, from the beagle and harrier packs of hounds that

Five newly-born Brown hare leverets (an exceptionally large litter) which were discovered on the verge of a well-used country lane by David Mason. The doe splits the leverets up within hours of birth to maximise their chances of avoiding predation, which makes this photograph all the more remarkable

hunt hares, as well as reliable sightings. The number of hares culled and shot by sportsmen is also taken into account.

Information from shooting estates suggests that the population of Brown hares has remained stable during the last ten years although this is not always the layman's view.

Country sports groups have worked for the survival of hares along with conservationists but obviously with different motives. Sportsmen have done their best to preserve the hare, as have many farmers for whom the conservation of the countryside and the creatures that live in it are important. The decline in hare numbers is reflected across Europe.

To carry out a survey on any population of hares in the world means counting them. Because of their very free-spirited nature, this is inevitably a difficult thing to do. In regions of Britain where there are few Brown hares, it is not easy to determine whether numbers are of a naturally established population or animals that have been introduced by well-meaning individuals. These releases not only distort the overall picture but also carry the risk of introducing disease to local areas from hares from other counties. It is almost impossible to carry out a detailed study of hares in their natural environment, yet they would not behave normally if kept under controlled conditions.

Monitoring desert hares

Desert conditions make counting species of hares even more difficult. Sightings here are almost non-existent because the animals are strictly nocturnal and hide from the heat of the sun during the daytime. Finding tracks in the sand is unreliable because the movement of other animals and people soon wipe them out, as does the wind.

The most reliable method of surveying desert hares discovered so far, is to search for droppings and count the number of places that faecal pellets are found. Many species of desert hares have declined for similar reasons to those that have caused the decline of the British Brown hare.

Modern farming methods have meant that camels and goats can now live in arid areas because food can be brought to them in 4x4 vehicles and water pumped from bore holes. As a result,

Right
The Brown hare has always been part of the countryside and has played an important role in our cultural heritage. It is hoped that various new farming initiatives will ensure the hare's future

Above
Hares are notoriously difficult to count, making population trends hard to monitor with any great accuracy

desert areas are now at risk of being over-grazed, reducing not only the availability of food for hares but also the cover they need to hide in. The presence of domestic livestock is also thought to attract more predators. There is little doubt that human interference with a hare's habitat anywhere in the world has probably had the greatest impact on population levels.

The hare throughout Western Europe

When EU subsidies were introduced in 1992 to provide the Arable Area Payment, farmers ploughed up as much ground as they could to claim the rewards. Likewise, headage payments for cattle and sheep resulted in an increase in the number of animals kept. Sheep numbers nearly doubled within a few years.

The only thing that seemed to benefit hares at that time was the introduction of set-aside on arable land. This is put to best use when it is utilised around the headlands of each field rather than putting a whole field into set-aside, thus spreading the areas in which hares could shelter and feed around the farm.

The EU requires member states under the Bio-diversity Action Plan (BAP) to help key species, including hares, and it is hoped to double the number of Brown hares in mainland Britain and the Irish hare in the whole of Ireland by 2010.

However, although the Brown hare is distributed across

Left
The EU policy of set-aside has been a very positive development for hares. It is one of the EU conservation initiatives that hopefully will double the number of Brown hares in mainland Britain (and the Irish hare in Northern Ireland) by 2010

mainland Britain, it is thought this increase will be difficult to achieve in pastoral areas where survival levels are poor and the increase is most needed. It is here that experts are undecided about how to reverse the downward trend. Agro-environmental schemes will be developed but what form they should take is debatable. Certainly a change in some farming practices might help. Block farming in which a single crop is sown over many acres, is bad for hares, who need variety in their diet.

Possibly more hares would be able to escape from silage fields if they were cut from the centre outwards. Leverets too would benefit if cattle pastures were not topped.

Farming patterns within the Countryside Stewardship Scheme – in which the government pays farmers to enhance and conserve the English landscape, its wildlife and history – should also benefit the hare. Management agreements usually last for ten years. Conservation measures include managing hay meadows, creating uncropped margins alongside arable fields, hedge restoration and moorland regeneration. New environmental schemes for farmers are to be introduced in 2005.

A similar pilot scheme, the Arable Stewardship Scheme, was introduced in the West Midlands and East Anglia in 1998 to promote the use of beetle banks, conservation headlands and over-winter stubble. It was adopted by many estates with great effect as a way of increasing populations of wild game birds. It has also benefited the hare.

Beetle Banks

These uncultivated strips of ground left in arable fields are called 'Beetle Banks' (see above). They are an environmental tool used by organic farmers and those conserving wildlife and wild gamebird stocks. They act as a haven for insects and provide a diverse source of plants for hares to feed on and shelter in.

163

Above
A beautifully-camouflaged
Brown hare lies in its form in
winter stubble

Detailed records of all species have been kept and the Game Conservancy Trust reports that hare numbers on farms that adopted the scheme are increasing in East Anglia (where there was already a sizeable population) compared with non-agreement farms where there was a decrease. This rise is due to use of the shelter areas, less disturbance and the greater variety of plants for hares to feed on. Numbers are said to be up by about 30%, more on some farms, although the rise in the population of Brown hares in the West Midlands, where there were fewer, was not significant. However, 2003 seemed to be a good year for hares anyway and it is a known fact that hare populations follow a fluctuating cycle so maybe they are at their natural peak in East Anglia at the moment.

Contradictory as it may seem, it is certain that banning hare coursing or hare hunting will be detrimental to the revival of the hare. About 1,500 are killed by hunting each year but thousands more survive because the hunters and coursers do all they can to preserve the hare and its habitat.

The Burns Inquiry and hares

The Government's Burns Inquiry conducted in 1999 into the impact of hunting with dogs in England and Wales endorsed this fact in its report as follows: 'Because hare numbers tend to be maintained at high levels in areas where hunting and coursing occur, the impact [of a hunting ban] might well be that, in the absence of other changes, the population would decline in those areas. This would partly result from a loss of suitable habitat, but also in a few areas, from the shooting of hares to deter poaching and illegal coursing.' In other words, fieldsports, which at first sight seem the biggest threat, are in fact one of the hares' greatest allies.

Illegal coursing will never be stopped by legislation. If those who now preserve hares on their land are not allowed to enjoy their sport then many hares will be culled, partly because of the damage they do but mainly because they are sure to attract the attentions of the very undesirable characters who participate in illegal hare coursing activities. In many areas landowners already shoot hares regularly with a rifle, often at night, in order to keep numbers low enough to deter illegal hare coursing, and this must have a big but unmeasurable impact on hare populations across the country. Many more hares escape than are caught by organised coursing but it is not known how many are accounted for by illegal coursing.

The Brown hare does best where there is a mixture of crops being grown. Unlike the less demanding Mountain and Irish hares, the Brown hare is a fussy feeder and needs variety

Cheshire Brown Hare Group

Brown hares once flourished across Britain but they now tend to be concentrated in certain areas. In 1999/2000 the Cheshire Brown Hare Group undertook a survey of farms and the results indicated that hares have declined in Cheshire. The estimated hare population in the county then stood at 6,133, which represents a density of 2.41 per square kilometre. However, in places such as the Wiltshire and Berkshire Downs, Lincolnshire, East Anglia, Yorkshire and parts of eastern Scotland, hares can still be found in pest proportions. In these areas shoots are organised in February to reduce the level and as many as 400 to 500 may be culled a day in this manner.

Because of the sharp decline of the Brown hare in so many areas since the 1960s, a biodiversity action plan has been put into place to encourage hares back into areas where they once thrived. The suggested action plan to increase the population of

Brown hares will not be applied to Northern Ireland as the Brown hare is not indigenous there and competes with the native Irish hare.

It is also proposed to review the use of legislation relating to the shooting and selling of hares.

Hares and modern farming practice

Despite the welcome aid of conservation grants and subsidies, the hare still has to contend with larger and faster farm machinery The fact that they crouch down and rely on camouflage for protection in these circumstances amounts to a form of suicide. Leverets are most at risk. An example of this happened recently when a litter of six new born leverets were inadvertently run over by a farmer driving his tractor along the 'tram lines', the widely-used tractor-sized gaps which farmers increasingly leave in their crops.

The Brown hare does best where there is a mixture of crops being grown. Unlike the less demanding Mountain and Irish hares, the Brown hare is a fussy feeder and needs variety, preferring lush new growth. Monoculture does little to help hares. While grass alone can sustain a hare through the winter, that is not enough to keep it in good condition during the breeding season. Throughout the Spring and Summer they need a variety of herbaceous plants to stay in peak condition. Once they could find this in the old pastures but no longer in the modern grass leys. Hares do not like sharing their feeding grounds with farm livestock.

Leverets are at great risk when the grass is cut for silage. It is now policy on many stock farms to regularly top the coarse tufts of grass left on land grazed by cattle. These are a favourite place for leverets to lay in. Topping the tufts not only deprives them of a hiding place but they are also likely to get cut up by the blades of the mower. Another factor is that there are no set-aside payment for grassland as there is on arable farms. This scheme was instigated to take land out of production, leaving it fallow so that weeds could grow and the vegetation could be left untouched and this has definitely helped the hare in arable areas. It is hoped that in future there will be more uptake of the

Unexpected result

Modern farming methods are partly blamed for the decline in the hare population, which makes it all the more surprising that, in East Anglia, where there has probably been most changes in cropping patterns and land preparation, the Brown hare still thrives.

Conversely in Devon and Cornwall, where farming methods have probably changed least, hare populations are at an all-time low

new flexible set-aside scheme, instead of rotational set-aside. This would allow set-aside fields to be left in place for two years which would lead to a greater variety of plants becoming established, thereby helping the hare.

Perhaps the biggest clue as to why East Anglia is still a stronghold for the Brown hare is that it is probably the most intensively keepered area in Britain and this is where they are still thriving. The ideal habitat and environment for gamebirds is also well suited to hares.

The Allerton Project

The Allerton project at Loddington in Leicestershire implemented by the Game Conservancy Trust combined habitat improvement and sympathetic farming with game keeping activities. This experiment was initiated to find out what impact farming and predator control has on game and other species of birds and mammals. In 1992 when the project began there were less than a dozen hares on the 333 hectare (824 acre) estate and by 2000 there were about 120. However, while the farming policies remained unchanged, keepering activities ceased in

Below
A Brown hare returning to its form at dawn. Hares will never again be such a source of superstition and myth as they have been in the past, thanks to modern scientific research and wildlife film-making

2001 and hare numbers have considerably declined since then. The winter count of hares for 2003 was less than 40. All this points to the fact that predation is a major threat and that gamekeepers control the hare's predators. One hundred years ago there were 23,000 gamekeepers: now there are less than 5,000.

If the day ever comes when gamebird shooting is restricted and most of the game keepers are made redundant, it will inevitably have a big impact on hare survival.

It is proposed that hare surveys should be carried out across the country at intervals, although records from coursing, hunting and shooting have always given a good indication of the position. It is usually field sportsmen who are first to notice any changes in the population of their quarry.

A delicate balance

It is to be hoped that sympathetic farming and the utilisation of conservation schemes will help to reverse the downward trend in hare numbers. Further research needs to be carried out to assess the effects on hare populations of agricultural activities such as crop-cutting dates and methods.

A hare's need for solitude

With the curious exception of airports, hares do not generally tolerate disturbance. They do not adapt to urbanisation and are rarely found in the vicinity of regularly-used public footpaths

Hares do not like disturbance. They do not adapt to urbanisation and are rarely found in the vicinity of regularly-used public footpaths. New laws on open access, the so-called right to roam, may well prove to have a detrimental affect on the distribution and general welfare of hares.

Hares can never again be such a source of superstition and myth as they have been in the past. Modern scientific research, technology that provides concrete information about the universe and a British population that is becoming far removed from countryside matters has led to a detached rational and, perhaps, clinical approach to all things. As a result, much of the mystery and romance is now missing and a hare is regarded as a less 'magical' creature: it is now just a hare.

Let us at least hope that hares will always be part of our countryside, even if they are no longer part of our culture.

The image of a natural survivor: a Brown hare in a Norfolk field of winter wheat. Autumn-sown cereals provide hares with a nourishing supply of food throughout the winter

Acknowledgements

When I started researching this book about hares I never anticipated how much help I would be given by so many people. I have been lent books, sent clippings from newspapers and magazines and received countless helpful phone calls, faxes, disks and emails. It was only as a last resort that I turned to the internet in my quest for specific information.

I have picked the brains of many experts, from scientists and conservationists to farmers and gamekeepers, and talked informally about hares with many others whose names I cannot now recall. To all of them, named and unnamed, I am deeply indebted.

I greatly appreciate the kindness of the many land-owners who gave permission for my husband David to take his photographs of hares on their land.

I wish to thank, most sincerely, the following people:

Gordon Anderson (Countryside Alliance, Ireland), Miss M. Birkbeck (Norfolk), Tim Bonner (Countryside Alliance), Duncan Bridges (Manx Wildlife Trust), John Burton (World Land Trust), George and Stephen Crouch (Sussex Game), Tom Greeves (Three Hares Project), Shelagh Jenkyns (Ludlow), Chris Knights (Norfolk), Jan Millington (Yorkshire), Paula Minchin (Holkham Estate), Declan O'Donovan (Dip. H.Ed., B.Sc.) in Dubai, Judith Prost (Central Administrator at the St Melangell Centre, Wales), Ted Roberts (retired kennel huntsman with the Wiltshire and Infantry Beagles), Alex Schwab, and Regina and Maria Christen (Switzerland), Katherine Whitwell, FRCV, (Newmarket), Martin Wright (Assistant Curator of the Salisbury and South Wiltshire Museum), Liz Woodall (Ludlow), Bernie O'Donovan and his friends Tony, Martin and Tom from County Cork, Ireland.

I also wish to thank the following Head Gamekeepers:
Colin Adamson (Burncastle, Scotland)
Duane Downing (Little Massingham)
Gerald Gray (Hilborough)
Robert Hall (Houghton)
Simon Lester (Holkham)
Jonathan Sharman (Narborough)
Jimmy Oswald (retired keeper from Glen Tanar, Scotland)

And finally, I wish to thank the beagle and harrier packs and the coursing clubs for permission to photograph them.

Epitaph on a hare

WILLIAM COWPER (1731-1800)

Here lies, whom hound did ne'er pursue,
Nor swifter greyhound follow,
Whose foot ne'er tainted morning dew,
Nor ear heard huntsman's halloo;

Old Tiney, surliest of his kind,
Who, nursed with tender care,
And to domestic bounds confined,
Was still a wild Jack hare.

Though duly from my hand he took
His pittance every night,
He did it with a jealous look,
And, when he could, would bite.

His diet was of wheaten bread,
And milk, and oats, and straw;
Thistles, or lettuces instead,
With sand to scour his maw.

On twigs of hawthorn he regaled,
On pippins' russet peel,
And, when his juicy salads fail'd,
Sliced carrot pleased him well.

A turkey carpet was his lawn,
Whereon he loved to bound,
To skip and gambol like a fawn,
And swing his rump around.

His frisking was at evening hours,
For then he lost his fear,
But most before approaching showers,
Or when a storm drew near.

Eight years and five round rolling moons
He thus saw steal away,
Dozing out his idle noons,
And every night at play.

I kept him for his humour's sake,
For he would oft beguile
My heart of thoughts that made it ache,
And force me to a smile.

But now beneath his walnut shade
He finds his long last home,
And waits, in snug concealment laid,
Till gentler Puss shall come.

He, still more aged, feels the shocks
From which no care can save,
And, partner once of Tiney's box,
Must soon partake his grave.

Bibliography

Aesop, *Fables, The Hare and the Tortoise* (p.115)

Aldrovandus (Aldrovandi), Ulysses (b.1522) *De Quadrupedib. Digitatis Viviparis, libri tres, et de quadrupedib. digitatis oviparis, libri duo* (p.114)

Allerton Project, *Where the Birds Sing*, 2002 (p.168)

Arrian (Flavius Arrianus), *On Hunting Hares*, pub. 125 AD (p.136)

Baily's Magazine of Sports and Pastimes (p.40)

Bible, The (pp.4, 74, 104, 113)

Blaine, Delabere P., *An Encyclopaedia of Rural Sports, or, a Complete account (historical, practical, and descriptive) of Hunting, Shooting, Fishing, Racing etc.* Longman, Orme, Brown, Green & Longman 1840 (p.114)

Burns Inquiry, The, *A Committee of Inquiry into Hunting with Dogs in England & Wales*, chaired by Lord Burns, 1999-2000. Final Report, The Stationery Office, 2000 (pp.164-165)

Burns, Robbie, *The Wounded Hare*, a poem sent to Mrs. Dunlop 21st April 1789 (p.4)

Carroll, Lewis, *Alice's Adventures in Wonderland* (pp.6, 113, 114)

Cobbett, William, *Rural Rides*, first published by the author, 1830 (p.40)

Cowper, William, *Epitaph on a Hare* (pp.4, 45, 52, 82)

Daniel, Rev. B. (p.79)

Domesday-book, The (p.39)

Evans, G. Ewart, and D. Thompson, *The Leaping Hare*, Faber & Faber, 1972

Gentleman's Magazine (p.83)

Gesner (Gessner), Conrad (1516-1565), *Historia Animalium Liber I: de Quadrupedibus Viviparis*, pub.1563 (p.114)

Gladstone, Hugh S., *Record Bags and Shooting Records*, HF & G Witherby, 1922

Glasse, Hannah, *The Art of Cookery Made Plain and Easy*, 1747 (p.127)

Goldsmith, Oliver (p.4)

Greeves, Dr. Tom, MA PhD, The Three Hares Project, a report in Dartmoor Magazine, Winter 1991 (and see websites) (p.112)

Grew, Dr. Nehemiah (1641-1712), *Musæum Regalis Societatis or a Catalogue and Description of the Natural and Artificial Rarities belonging to the Royal Society and preserved at Gresham Colledge*, pub. 1681 (p.114)

Grimm Brothers, *The Three Brothers*, 1937 edition illustrated by Ruth Koser-Michaels (p.101)

MacPherson, Revd. H.A., Lascelles, The Hon. Gerald, Richardson, Charles, Gibbons, J.S., Longman, G.H., Kenney Herbert, Col., *The Hare: Natural History; Shooting; Coursing; Hunting: Cookery*, (Fur, Feather & Fin series), Longman 1896. Illustrated by G. D. Giles, A. Thorburn and C. Whymper (p.126)

Manley MA, J. J., *Notes on Game and Game Shooting*, pub. Bazaar Office, London, c.1880 (pp.84, 130)

Merrymet magazine 2003 (p.106)

Millington, Jan (p.106) (article in *Merrymet magazine* 2003)

Pepys, Samuel, *The Diary of Samuel Pepys* (p.108)

Queens University Belfast, Northern Ireland Irish Hare Survey 2004, published September 2004: www.quercus.ac.uk/pages/news_hares.htm

Tegner, Henry, *Wild Hares*, pub. John Baker, London, 1969 (p.12)

The Sporting Magazine, 1830 (p.145)

Venner, Dr. Tobias (1577-1660), *Via Recta ad Vitam Longam. Or, a Plaine Philosophical Demonstration of the Nature, Faculties, and Effects of all such things as by way of nourishments make for the preservation of health* Printed by R. Bishop, 2nd ed. 1638. (p.126)

Webb, Cecil *A Hare about the House*, Hutchinson & Co Ltd, 1955

Whitwell, Katherine E., FRCVS, *Dysautonomia as a cause of death in wild hares in the UK.* Association of Veterinary Teachers and Research Workers, 30th March 1994, abstract (pp.94-96)

More cases of leporine dysautonomia (letter), Veterinary Record, 134, 223-224 (1994)

Yeats, W. B., *Two Songs of a Fool* – poem (p.84)

LEGISLATION

Game Act 1831 (pp.117, 121, 122)
Game Preservation (Special Protection for Irish Hares) Order (Northern Ireland), Statutory Rule No. 534 of 2003
Ground Game Act 1880 (pp.40, 123)
Hares Act 1848 (p.122)
Hares Protection Act 1892 (pp.118, 124)
Larceny Act 1861 (p.122)
Theft Act 1968 (p.117)
Wildlife and Countryside Act 1981 (p.123)
Witchcraft Act 1736 (p.105)

WEBSITES

Allerton Project, The www.fwag.org.uk/html/allerSimple.html
Arable Stewardship Scheme www.defra.gov.uk/erdp/schemes/pre_erdp/arable.htm
Association of Lurcher Clubs www.users.daelnet.co.uk/lurchers
British Brown Hare Preservation Society www.brown-hare-preservation.co.uk
Burns Inquiry, The, 1999 - www.huntinginquiry.gov.uk
Cheshire Brown Hare Group – www.cheshire-biodiversity.org.uk/mammal-bhare.htm
Countryside Stewardship Scheme www.defra.gov.uk/erdp/schemes/css/default.htm
Game Conservancy Trust – www.gct.org.uk
Masters of Harriers and Beagles Association - www.amhb.org.uk
National Coursing Club - www.nationalcoursingclub.org
Northern Ireland Environment and Heritage Service www.ehsni.gov.uk
Northern Pagan Archive - hometown.aol.co.uk/bonawitch
Queens University Belfast – Irish hare survey project - www.quercus.ac.uk/pages/news_hares.htm
Three Hares Project www.chrischapmanphotography.com/hares/page1.htm
UK Biodiversity Action Plan - www.ukbap.org.uk. - links to local and university BAP sites.
World Conservation Union (IUCN) - www.iucn.org

Index